EAT YOUR WAY SLIM & HEALTHY

BRIDGET DAVIS

EAT YOUR WAY SLIM & HEALTHY

SUGAR FREE ✓ + DAIRY FREE ✓ + GLUTEN FREE ✓

murdoch books

Sydney | London

**This book is dedicated to my rock,
my best friend, my husband.
You make me want to be a better person.**

CONTENTS

Dinner 153

Treats **213**

Preserves **245**

Veg **255**

FOREWORD

Liz Kaelin MSc, RD

Five years ago I started a business connecting local chefs, cafes and restaurants to the catering needs of customers. A mutual acquaintance introduced me to Bridget Davis, a professional chef who had spent most of her life in kitchens and had gained a reputation for being one of the best chefs in Australia. Bridget was a brand ambassador for Grove Avocado Oil and Lenovo (in addition to being an incredible chef, Bridget was also highly social media savvy), had given a TEDx talk at Macquarie University, and was regularly sought after by Google to cater their most prestigious and important events.

At the time, I was a practising dietitian who knew food and how it affects the body, but very little of the hospitality business and the mentality of chefs. From the moment I met Bridget, I was struck by her kindness, passion, enthusiasm, and infectious positive energy. She freely gave me her time and expertise, although she was a busy professional with several businesses and a mum of small children to boot. Through Bridget's patience and guidance, I shifted my knowledge from one of medical nutrition therapy to learning about the hospitality business, and slowly built a business that after five years was turning over $1 million in revenue before being sold in July 2017. Much of the credit is due to Bridget's contribution.

Fast forward six months later and as a 'fan' of Bridget's Facebook page, I begin to see Bridget post healthy recipes. But not just any healthy recipes – these dishes spanned the world's cuisines and were packed full of fresh garden vegetables, aromatic herbs, exotic spices and lean meats. The recipes were incredibly inventive, yet dead simple – so important for today's world when time is at a premium for all of us. The ingredients of the recipes were highly accessible (aside from a few speciality items) and required minimum prep time. As I observed Bridget pump out recipe after mouth-watering recipe: Korean-spiced beef with pickled cucumber, one-sheet-pan chicken and asparagus, Jamaican-jerk fish curry with roasted cauliflower rice (now I'm getting hungry!) I noticed a trend. The recipes contained no gluten and no dairy – which is becoming a more popular health trend – but Bridget was also not adding any sugar or fat to her recipes. The result was pure, 'clean', delicious meals – 'real' food which was tasty, easy to prepare and really, really healthy.

Bridget's recipes are primarily focused on 'gut' health. Simply put, our 'gut', or gastrointestinal tract, is an organ system within humans which takes in food and digests it to extract and absorb energy and nutrients. The incredible complexity of the gut and its importance to our overall health is a topic of increasing research in the medical community. Numerous studies in the past two decades have demonstrated links between gut health and the immune system, mood, mental health, autoimmune diseases, endocrine disorders, skin conditions and cancer.

The gastrointestinal tract contains some 4,000 different strains of 'flora' (bacteria) which have diverse roles in maintenance of immune health and metabolism.

But back to Bridget's recipes. Her style of cooking and eating promotes gut health on various levels:

No added sugar: A diet high in added sugars can decrease the amount of good bacteria in your gut. This imbalance can cause increased sugar cravings, which can damage your gut still further. High amounts of refined sugars, particularly high-fructose corn syrup, have been linked to increased inflammation in the body, which in turn can be a precursor to a number of diseases and even cancers.

No gluten: Gluten is a type of protein that is found in wheat. Certain features of gluten make it more likely to induce immune responses than other proteins. One key difference is that gluten is less amenable to being broken down by the enzymes that normally digest proteins. Another factor is gluten's propensity to bind to certain proteins in immune cells that normally detect pathogens. This can lead to a cascade of events that result in the activation of various types of immune cells; in other words, gluten causes inflammation. Every person is different, and some gut microbes are more susceptible than others to gluten proteins, but for those who suffer gut issues, a gluten-free diet can be a step in the right direction to reduce the risk of tummy troubles.

No dairy: While small amounts of certain types of dairy are not harmful to the gut, dairy milk is meant for baby cows, not humans. Dairy contains the nutrition calves need to grow, so it is full of many important nutrients such as calcium, vitamin D, riboflavin (B2), vitamin B12, potassium, and phosphorus. But since modern milk almost always comes from recently pregnant cows, it also contains bovine (cow) hormones that are thought to be one of the reasons that dairy consumption has been found to be associated with increased rates of risk of certain cancers. Moreover, as infants, our bodies produce a digestive enzyme called lactase, which breaks down lactose from mother's milk. But as we grow up, many of us lose the ability to do that. This can strain and distress our gastrointestinal tract, particularly for non-Caucasians. Fermented dairy, such as yoghurt and cottage cheese, is always recommended over other dairy sources due to its probiotic properties.

No added fats: High-fat diets are linked to unfavourable alterations to gut microbiota. These alterations are linked not only to obesity but to subsequent development of chronic diseases due to increased gut permeability and inflammation. Gut permeability or 'leaky gut' is a condition in which the lining of the small intestine becomes damaged, causing undigested food particles, toxic waste products and bacteria to 'leak' through the intestines and flood the bloodstream. Plus, no added fats means you are drastically reducing the calories of a given dish, meaning you can either eat more so you stay fuller longer, or lose weight due to the creation of a calorie deficiency (provided this is done in conjunction with your diet holistically over time).

High in dietary fibre: Dietary fibre acts as a 'prebiotic' – a substrate by which a 'probiotic' can feed and therefore proliferate. In layman's terms, fibre acts as food for healthy bacteria, so the more fibre you eat from those delicious veggie-laden recipes, the more your healthy gut flora can grow. A low-fibre diet can deprive our beneficial gut microbes of the food they need to flourish, which could offset the bacterial balance and reduce its diversity.

I messaged Bridget to ask her about her new recipes, impressed as always with how delicious and healthy they were (I've tried out more than a few!). As a dietitian, I have witnessed first-hand how difficult it is for the average person to eat more healthfully. Not only is unhealthy food readily accessible (and humans were built to feast or famine, hence us holding body fat as we prepare for the 'lean' times) but people want to know the answer to the most basic of questions: 'I know what I shouldn't eat; but What DO I eat??'

Look no further, foodie friends, as Bridget has solved your problem. A cookbook not only designed to heal your gut, but to please your palate, wallet and waistline, with time left over to spend with your family at the end of the night. Bridget's way of eating comes complete with recommendations for the best gut-healing products and time-saving tips so that you can meal prep with ease.

As a dietitian I cannot recommend Bridget's recipes more highly. I love food and I do not deprive myself of a good slice of cheesy, doughy pizza or a lovely frosted cupcake now and again. But for those needing to kickstart their health, or wanting to incorporate a healthier way of eating into their everyday lives most of the time (what we call the 80/20 rule), Bridget's keen knack for flavour profiles will never leave you deprived, will satisfy even the toughest cravings and will leave your gut happy, healthy and ready for its next (healthy and tasty!) Bridget-inspired recipe.

Liz Kaelin MSc, RD

INTRODUCTION

I was in trouble; I knew it. I'd stopped looking at myself in the mirror, and the thought of leaving my house and going out in public filled me with terror. Self-confined to my bedroom, paralysed by insecurities, I was too ashamed even to let my own family see me. Depression and anxiety had taken up firm residence in my mind and spirit.

It was February 2018. My weight and health were out of control. I'd get changed with the lights off and wore clothes were three sizes too big for me, so I could hide those parts of my body I couldn't bear to look at or acknowledge. I was severely overweight and miserable.

Sometime a few years' previously, I had convinced myself that being a middle-aged married mother of three meant being overweight, frumpy, bloated and uncomfortable, grumpy, moody, and depressed. It was just part of getting older – there wasn't much I could do to slow it down or stop it. Thanks to a slowing metabolism and being genetically big boned, I self-diagnosed, this was my lot. I should just accept it. People in my immediate and extended family were big, especially the women, so of course I was going to be big as well.

Together with my constantly negative inner voice, these thought patterns had become my personal theme-song of dislike and distaste, both for myself and the extra weight I was carrying. Combined with always feeling tired to the point of exhaustion, and never feeling comfortable or allowing myself to feel beautiful, no matter what I wore, my weight was not just taking a toll on me, it also impacted how I communicated with my family and friends.

Being overweight, unhealthy and painfully inflamed caused me to feel depressed. Depression caused me to seek out comfort foods such as chocolate and lollies, breads, cakes, bagels, burgers and deep-fried foods – they were my all-encompassing, but fleeting, feel-good fix.

The fix never lasted long. As soon as I had eaten the packet of cookies; family-sized bag of potato chips; or extra-large burger combo with fries, chicken nuggets and a milkshake, I'd ridicule myself for being an undisciplined fat slob. I was on a vicious merry-go-round, with no idea how I could get myself off this terrible ride, physically or mentally.

I repulsed myself. I hated myself and the woman I'd let myself become. Enough was enough.

It was the release of my first cookbook. I was at my lowest point. With all the time spent hiding away from the rest of the world in my bedroom, I'd managed to write a manuscript for a cookbook. When this cookbook was accepted to be published, I was given the opportunity to appear on national television in Australia to promote my work.

To say that this prospect filled me with dread was an understatement of epic proportions. I'd heard that the camera puts on 10 kilos (22 pounds) – this would cause me to look like an elephant in a chef's jacket. I was at my heaviest, weighing more than when I was 9 months' pregnant, so television was going to tip the scales, figuratively and physically.

I was paralysed with fear. 'Fatty boom-sticks', as I so unaffectionately referred to myself, would have to appear on primetime television and try to convince people that buying her cookbook and eating her food were actually satisfying. I felt so unsatisfied with my own life and journey with food.

My irrational yet rational fear, exacerbated by my uneasiness of being seen in public in my physical state, finally spurred me to act.

As a food-obsessed chef with more than 30 years' experience in professional kitchens worldwide, I know how to make food taste delicious. For as long as I've been picking up a whisk and a spoon, I've been able to take simple ingredients and turn them into something delectable that excites people's palates. My style of cooking was an indulgent journey through fat, sugar, salt and flour, thanks to my quest to conquer flavours above all else – you might say it was my superpower.

On such a mission, and with a head full of misinformation about myself, I had chosen to ignore my body. I treated food for the sole purpose of pleasure. I knew how to cook, but I had no idea how to eat.

I began to research. All that time I spent alone in my room meant I had ample opportunity to read and discover what other people in my situation had done to lose weight and heal their bodies. Through endless hours of research, I kept returning to the concept of gut health. Having a healthy gut could help, not just with weight loss, but also with other areas of your life such as energy, mood swings, depression and anxiety, sleep patterns, diabetes, PCOS, metabolic illnesses, heart disease, high blood pressure, and bloating and inflammation.

One of my family members had taken a gut health program with some success, so I decided to jump on board. This program came with a meal plan, which I attacked with gusto, only to find myself bored out of my mind within days and contemplating giving up. The food was so bland; it tasted terrible. How could anyone stick to this healthy change long term,

if the food was almost unbearable to eat? It wasn't sustainable, let alone interesting.

Armed with my experience as a chef, and my superpower of taking simple ingredients and making them taste good, I dumped the mind-numbingly boring gut health program. I applied my knowledge of cooking and flavour to the universal principles of gut health – removing all sugar (including honey, maple and syrups) from my diet, along with gluten and wheat products, as well as seriously minimising dairy.

Combining this with small amounts of good-quality protein and large amounts of fresh vegetables, I began to create my own bespoke gut healthy recipes, which any chef or foodie would love to eat.

Suddenly, things started to make sense. Not only was I enjoying food, and even looking forward to eating what I was creating and cooking, but the weight was dropping off me.

Over a 5½ month period, I shed nearly 30 kilograms (66 pounds) – a feat I thought impossible for a woman in her mid-forties. My husband Mahe'i was so impressed with my dramatic weight loss and health gain that he jumped on the bandwagon too. He shed 15 kilos (33 pounds) in 30 days. The biggest win for us was: not only did he lose weight, but he stopped snoring after only 3 days of going dairy, sugar and gluten free.

During this period, I felt better than I had in decades. My mood swings were gone, bloating was no longer an issue, and I had more energy than I knew what to do with. My hair and nails were strong, my skin cleared up and was glowing, and I found a newfound joy in meeting people and getting about town.

I no longer felt depressed or anxious, and I enjoyed full nights of uninterrupted quality sleep, thanks to Mahe'i not snoring and a happy content digestive system when I went to bed. My gut was no longer keeping me awake with bloating, pain and discomfort.

I felt like a new woman, recharged, vibrant and ready to take on the world. My brain fog had disappeared. I had clarity of mind and a zing in my step. Within those 5½ months, everything I achieved was through changing my diet. I hadn't once stepped into a gym or exercised. I finally understood the age-old saying: food is either our greatest medicine or our biggest poison.

My goal before appearing on television to promote my first cookbook was to lose 10 kilograms (22 pounds) in 30 days. When my TV slot arrived, I'd lost 12 kilograms (26½ pounds). During those 30 days, I'd been so busy writing healthy recipes and enjoying my new healthy lifestyle, I'd forgotten to buy myself a smaller chef's jacket. When I appeared on television, my dramatic weight loss was covered by a jacket that was two sizes too big for me. But I knew what I had achieved, and that's what really mattered.

My newly discovered energy resulted in an avalanche of healthy recipes. I began to share my recipes with folks online, thinking that maybe someone else might benefit from these ideas, too. I was enjoying my journey of eating satisfying yet healthy food so much, I wanted everyone to feel as good as I did, while eating deliciously as well.

Combining the chef's code of 'flavour forward food' with my new approach of 'food as medicine', I wanted to turn the idea of healthy food on its head. Why couldn't we drool over a recipe without sugar, gluten or dairy, which wasn't deep-fried in oil. Why couldn't we eat chicken scotch eggs for breakfast, and combine pickles with a curry for dinner?

I was overwhelmed by the response I received after posting my simple and healthy, yet incredibly delicious, recipes online. At first, I tried to send out individual messages and PDFs to everyone who asked for a recipe, but quickly realised this was not physically possible. Within a matter of a weeks, I was getting more than 500 requests per recipe every day.

Due to this unprecedented demand, I developed *Bridget's Healthy Kitchen* on Facebook and online, and our sites have grown into an incredible community of like-minded people. In our private group *Bridget's Healthy Kitchen Family*, we share ideas, recipes and shopping tips, as well as support, mentor and inspire each other. I run live cooking classes a couple of times a week on my YouTube channel, where you can catch up on my videos and healthy masterclasses.

If you were to say to me that I would be writing the foreword to my first healthy cookbook, I would have thought it crazy. But now that I've experienced how good food can make you feel, and how satisfying healthy food can be, I am totally converted to this new lifestyle.

My hope is to teach you the fundamentals of healthy cooking because when you know how to cook, you regain control of your diet and your life. You become the master of your health and wellness journey, because you have the ways, means and knowledge of what to cook and how to cook it – without losing taste and satisfaction.

I created these recipes with both you and me in mind. They are a direct result of what I ate to regain my health. Every recipe you see in this book started on my dinner plate. I was the guinea pig, trying out and testing all the recipes on my body and my taste buds, before introducing them to my family.

How do I feel? Your health is your wealth, so I feel like the richest person on Earth. I want to help others feel this good because there is nothing like this sweet feeling. I am high on life and fuelled by goodness.

I hope these recipes are as good for you as they are for me.

Love,

Bridget

THESE ARE A FEW OF MY FAVOURITE THINGS

Ingredients and staples

HERBS One of the cornerstones of adding flavour to food is with the use of herbs. Culinary herbs are categorised as the leaves, seeds, roots, buds or flowers of edible plants and come in many wonderful forms. I like to use fresh leaves like coriander, mint and basil. As well as fresh herbs, dried seeds and buds also make regular appearances but feel free to swap the herbs around if you don't like a particular herb.

The best way to store fresh herbs is to wash them under gently running cold water and the shake the bunches to remove any large water droplets. Wet a clean tea towel or cloth under cold water and wrap the herbs in the damp tea towel. Leave the herbs in the vegetable crisper or at the bottom of the fridge, rewetting the tea towel every couple of days.

SPICES Don't let the word spice confuse you. A spice is not necessarily spicy (hot) but it is an aromatic element added to food to give flavour. Spices, much like herbs, are plant-based and come in many forms but are commonly found ground for convenience. Some of my favourite spices are combinations, and within the foundation recipes I have given you some of my most beloved spice blends (page 42).

Buy spices in small quantities so that they remain as fresh as possible and use within 12 months. Store the spices in airtight jars or sealed containers for optimum flavour.

APPLE CIDER VINEGAR (with the mother) Apple cider vinegar not only tastes good, but it's very good for gut health as it helps to balance the body's pH levels, especially when the mother is still in the vinegar. The mother means that all the beneficial bacteria are still in the vinegar as it is unfiltered, unpasteurised and unrefined. Choose an organic and naturally fermented vinegar, if possible, for optimum benefits.

TAMARI SAUCE Tamari may look like soy sauce but it is a lighter more refined version of soy sauce and is gluten and wheat free. Tamari is the by-product of making miso so it tastes a lot more delicate than most soy sauces. If possible, choose a low-sodium tamari and make sure to check the ingredients labels as not all tamari sauces are created equal. Avoid tamari that has added sugar and sodium.

Tamari can be purchased in most good supermarkets either in the health food or gluten-free section.

KOMBU Try not to judge a book by its cover when it comes to the understated beauty that is kombu. Kombu is dried kelp or seaweed and is primarily used to make stocks and broths. It comes in large dried sheets that look rather leathery. I don't suggest trying to eat it whole; its primary function is to add flavour to stocks. In terms of its benefits, kombu has many including aiding digestion and regulating metabolism and thyroid function, and can give the feeling of fullness so it's helpful with weight loss. It is also high in iron and can help reduce bloating, gas and even constipation.

You can purchase kombu at health food stores, in Asian grocery stores or online.

WAKAME Another form of edible sea vegetables or seaweed is wakame. Sold dry in strips, flakes or ground, wakame is a great flavouring agent in food as well as having similar health benefits to kombu (see above). I add wakame strips to soups and rehydrate them and also add it to salads. I love using ground wakame (page 40) instead of salt to add that wonderful umami flavour to finished dishes.

You can purchase wakame at health food stores, in Asian grocery stores or online.

INULIN POWDER Inulin is a soluble fibre derived from chicory root so is amazingly good for us. This fine white powder is a prebiotic so improves gut health, can help relieve constipation, helps to curb your appetite and is 100% natural. It also has a slight sweetness to it, making it very user friendly. As it is a soluble fibre it does have laxative qualities if consumed excessively, so be aware.

You can find inulin powder at your health food store or online.

FIBRE SYRUP This clear liquid is the syrup equivalent of inulin powder (see above) and is a great replacement for honey, maple, rice malt syrup and agave. A natural prebiotic like inulin, the syrup is a soluble fibre so it will boost the fibre content of your cooking and aid gut health. It has a very low glycaemic index and is extremely low in calories, with only 5 calories per 100 ml (3½ fl oz)!

You can purchase fibre syrup online.

FRESH LEMON AND LIME Although we all know what fresh lemons and limes are, we should not underestimate their wonderful addition to food. With fresh being the only way to go here, the juice, flesh and zest can all be used for great results. Lemon and lime juice are used to marinate food and balance flavours and as a base to dressings. They are second to none. Zest is a powerhouse of pungent flavours and the goodness of a wedge

of citrus served with your meal is another way to get additional flavour into your food.

You can use lemons and limes interchangeably and when they are in abundance, juice and freeze in ice cube trays.

CHOPPED GINGER AND GARLIC Again, fresh is the only way to go here! Buy bulbs of garlic and rhizomes of fresh ginger and chop them in a small food processor so you have sealed containers of chopped ginger and garlic in your fridge at all times. This will speed up your cooking x10! Avoid pre-crushed ginger and garlic in the supermarket because they tend to be loaded with preservatives like sugar, gluten and sodium.

A major tip to speed up the ginger chopping process is that there is no need to peel your ginger. Roughly chop it, then place it into your food processor and blend until finely chopped. Fresh ginger and garlic will last for up to 2 weeks if stored correctly in the fridge.

HIMALAYAN SALT I use Himalayan as my choice of salt. This is because Himalayan salt has a few more trace elements than normal table salt and it tastes a darn sight better too. Regardless, go gently with adding salt to food as it's still sodium and over-consumption could make you feel bloated. It also causes you to retain water and can increase blood pressure. Check out my aromatic salt (page 45) for a great way to get more flavour into less salt.

NUTRITIONAL YEAST Don't confuse nutritional yeast with normal bakers' yeast. Nutritional yeast is a deactivated yeast that can be used as a food source; it is a popular cheese alternative for vegans and vegetarians. Yellow in colour with a strong and delicious flavour, it is called nutritional yeast because it is high in B vitamins and trace minerals, and is a good source of dietary fibre.

You can find nutritional yeast in your supermarket's health food aisle or in a health food store.

Favourite kitchen equipment and appliances

I'm not suggesting you rush out and purchase everything on my list here, but as I often get asked what I use in my own kitchen, I thought it could be helpful to share.

SMALL FOOD PROCESSOR I find a small food processor handy for making sauces, purées and mashes and chopping garlic and ginger. Most of the time I don't have enough ingredients to fill a normal-sized food processor, so the versatility of a small handheld one is not just budget friendly but it's also a great space saver in the kitchen. My small processor also has a stick blender and whisk attachment.

AIR FRYER I am an air fryer convert and cannot speak highly enough of them. They can cook a variety of foods quickly and without the need for any additional fats and oils. Food gets crispy and caramelised and whether I'm cooking sticky salmon or making cauliflower chips, the versatility and speed of this appliance is legendary. I use my air fryer almost every day and love the fact that it's easy to clean as well.

PRESSURE COOKER I never truly appreciated how great pressure cookers are until one long cold winter when I was working longer hours than usual and my pressure cooker rescued many a family dinner. Pressure cookers are able to take tough secondary cuts of meat that would normally take 6–10 hours to make enjoyable and turn them into a tender stew, pot roast or curry in an hour or less. With no need to add additional fats, oils or gluten, you have the world of comfort foods at your fingertips.

My pressure cooker is actually a multicooker that can also slow cook, steam, sear and reduce. If you are looking at buying a pressure cooker, you may want to consider a multicooker as it quite the versatile kitchen appliance.

REX PEELER/WIDE POTATO PEELER
It might seem strange that I have included a peeler into my favourites list, but the rex peeler or wide peeler is so much more than something to peel your carrots! It can be used to make thin strips or ribbons of vegetables quickly and safely and is easy to store as it just sits in your utensil draw. It's also known as a speed peeler because even if you are just peeling, it's super-fast thanks to its wide surface area.

NON-STICK, FLAT-BASED WOK I can't get enough of my wok and use it pretty much every single day. Its flat bottom means it can work on any type of cooktop and its non-stick interior means I don't have to add additional oil and fats when I'm cooking. A good-quality, non-stick wok can be used to stir-fry but I also use it for cooking most things that I would cook in a pot as the wide surface area cooks food faster and cleaning is so much easier.

MANDOLIN Look into the equipment stores of any professional kitchen and you will find a mandolin. A kitchen mandolin is a manually controlled slicer that can give you thin strips of nearly any vegetable or hard food. It comes with a set of different sized teeth so you can also grate, or make noodles or matchsticks. I use my mandolin to ever so thinly slice cabbage for slaw and zucchini (courgette) for chips and to make vegetable noodles. A word of warning though, make sure you use the finger guard to avoid any potential slips and cuts – speaking from experience!

VACUUM SEALER If you like to meal prep or prepare food in advance, you may want to look into purchasing a vacuum sealer. Sealing food and removing the air that surrounds it will double and sometimes triple the shelf life of fresh food when stored in the refrigerator and in some case will completely negate the need to freeze food. You can still freeze vacuum-sealed food which will triple or quadruple the shelf life.

HOW TO USE THIS BOOK

This cookbook was designed with you and me in mind. When I first started on my health journey I found that I was cooking and eating solo because it took some time to convince my husband to join me. Talking with people that I met online who were using and loving my recipes, I found they were experiencing the same so I continued to create recipes to serve one, which you will find is a common theme in this cookbook. These recipes are perfect serves for one diner to make sure you are getting the right nutrition and quantities of food for you to thrive on this style of eating. Some of the recipes with more than one serve were easier to create as a multiple so you can either share your meal with someone special or you have a spare meal for next time.

If you are cooking for more than one, congratulations! Sharing is caring and all you have to do is multiply the recipe quantities and then divide the food equally amongst the people you are serving. This works really well if you are meal prepping and organising these recipes for freezing or stocking up your fridge.

Sometimes it does take a while to convince others to join you, and that is completely OK, because what I discovered with my own husband was that once he realised that the weight was literally dropping off me and my health had improved ten-fold, he wanted in! I did not try to talk him into it, I let the results speak for me because some folks need a visual guide — seeing is believing. So even if you are like me and start this trip as a single rider, it won't be long before people will want to jump on the wagon with you. Welcome them with open arms and enjoy the ride together.

All the recipes in this book have been designed for optimum gut health. They use a concept known as mono eating which means you eat one vegetable and one protein at lunch and dinner. This helps your gut in the healing process. Breakfast consists of high protein options that will help to keep you feeling fuller longer, without overwhelming your digestive system.

These recipes are low calorie by nature; you should check with your healthcare professional before undertaking any low-calorie protocol.

If you would like more recipes simply log on to:
https://www.bridgetshealthykitchen.com

Use these symbols to quickly identify the main features of each recipe.

gluten free   sugar free   dairy free   fat free   no added fat   vegan

BASICS ARE YOUR FOUNDATION RECIPES.

Regardless of what meal plan you are on, be it gut health or simply healthy living, before you can build your healthy house you need to start with a solid foundation.

I champion the necessity of sauces, dressings and spice blends as well as having pre-chopped fresh garlic and ginger in the refrigerator at all times. Kombu water for soups and gravies, as well as ground wakame, make up the base of my foundation so then all I have to do is build the walls and roof for a fabulous meal in minutes.

I'm convinced that having some of these foundation recipes at your disposal is key. Meal prepping should be renamed foundation prepping because once you have some of these recipes ready to go, lunch or dinner is only minutes away.

Basics

Bridget's sticky sauce

When you hear the word sticky attached to food, it's hard to imagine it as not being gooey, delicious and syrupy. Such is the absolute case with this sticky sauce. It deserves its own recipe as opposed to just being part of another recipe. This sauce is a dream come true.

1 green apple, peeled, cored and diced

240 ml (8 fl oz) low-sodium tamari

120 ml (4 fl oz) apple cider vinegar

120 ml (4 fl oz) water

3 slices ginger

1 lime, zested and juiced

Place the apple in a small pot and add enough water so that it comes halfway up the apple. Bring to the boil and cook for 10 minutes, or until the apple is soft and the water has evaporated.

Blend the apple in a small food processor until smooth, then place into a pot.

Add the tamari, apple cider vinegar, water, ginger, lime zest and lime juice to the apple and whisk well to combine.

Bring the sauce to the boil, then reduce down to a rapid simmer. Cook for 10–15 minutes, or until the sauce has reduced down by half. You should still have about 240 ml (8 fl oz) of liquid once it has reduced down. Cool the sauce and store in a jar in the refrigerator for up to 2 months.

TIP There is a green apple in this sauce, so factor that in if you are strictly calorie counting. But as you only need a tablespoon or two for each portion you cook, the calorie content is extremely low – less than 5 calories per tablespoon.

TIP Use this sauce on everything. Marinate meat overnight in it. Slosh it through a stir-fry. Add it to minced (ground) meat as it cooks. Brush some on your chicken, beef or vegetables skewers. Marinate tofu in it. The world is your oyster. Go crazy and enjoy!

Oil-free pesto

This is a fantastic alternative to an oil-based pesto – the flavours of the basil and lemon really shine through.

60 g (2¼ oz/3 cups) basil leaves

12 g (½ oz/1 cup) flat-leaf (Italian) parsley leaves

1–2 lemons, juiced and zested

2 large garlic cloves, peeled

60 ml (2 fl oz/¼ cup) water

Himalayan salt and freshly ground black pepper.

Place the basil, parsley, juice of 1 lemon, garlic and water into a blender and blend on high for 30–60 seconds, or until the basil leaves are small and very well blended. If the pesto seems a bit dry, add a tablespoon of water at a time, blending between each addition until a thick sauce forms.

TIP Season the pesto with 1 teaspoon of salt and ½ teaspoon pepper and taste for flavour, adding more lemon juice or seasoning if required. Use drizzled through a salad, with fish, to flavour steamed vegetables, over roasted vegetables, with meat, through a soup or as a dip.

TIP Store this pesto in a sealed jar or container in the refrigerator. It will keep for up to 2 weeks if stored correctly.

Bridget's zesty dressing

Lemon and ginger is a wonderful combination and, combined with mint, it makes for a zesty fresh dressing that has no fat or sugar.

90 ml (3 fl oz) lemon juice

1 garlic clove, crushed

2 teaspoons crushed ginger

1 tablespoon sugar-free dijon mustard (I use Maille mustard), (optional)

pinch of Himalayan salt and freshly ground black pepper

60 ml (2 fl oz/¼ cup) water

1 small handful mint leaves, roughly chopped

½ green chilli, roughly chopped (optional)

Place all the ingredients into a small blender and pulse until well blended.

Taste the dressing for flavour, adding more lemon, water or salt and pepper to taste.

TIP This dressing is great through salads, over steamed vegetables or with fresh vegetables like cucumber.

TIP This delicious dressing will keep for at least 1 month if stored in a covered jar or container in the refrigerator.

Tamari and lime dipping sauce

I LOVE this dipping sauce for healthy breakfast patties, prawn dumplings and all manner of seafood and cooked vegetables.

200 ml (7 fl oz) low-sodium tamari

1 lime, juiced

1 large garlic clove, finely chopped

1 tablespoon grated ginger

1–2 pinches of chilli flakes, to taste

Mix together the ingredients in a bowl and taste for flavour, adding more lime juice and chilli to taste.

TIP Double the recipe and store this sauce in the fridge as it has great keeping qualities and will last for at least 1 month.

Saffron and star anise water

This is an aromatic and flavoursome broth that utilises so many fabulous flavours. It makes a great base for curries, tagines and soups.

20 threads (1 pinch) saffron strands

1 litre (35 fl oz/4 cups) cold water

8 star anise

2 heaped tablespoons roughly crushed cardamom pods

4 cinnamon quills

Make the water by soaking the saffron strands in 2 tablespoons of boiling water for 10 minutes.

In the meantime, bring a small pot to a gentle simmer with the water, star anise, crushed cardamom and cinnamon quills. Add the saffron strands and soaking liquid. Reduce the heat to very low and cook very gently for 30 minutes to allow the flavours time to infuse.

Leave the water to cool, then store in a covered jar or container in the refrigerator until required.

TIP This water will keep in the fridge for at least 1 month. Simply store in a covered jug, jar or container.

Kombu water

This liquid is my go-to stock for all my broths, soups and sauces. I ALWAYS have a couple of jars in my fridge, ready to make a quick, tasty lunch or dinner. This water is easy to make and so wonderful to include in your culinary repertoire.

2 pieces of kombu, 20 cm x 20 cm (7.8 in x 7.8 in) each

5 litres (169 litres/ 20 cups) cold water

Place the kombu into a large pot and pour over the cold water. Bring the pot to a simmer, then reduce the heat to very low.

Allow the liquid to gently steep for 5 hours over a low temperature, then cool.

Pour the liquid into glass jars and add the kombu. Store the water in the fridge for up to 1 month.

TIP Kombu is dried seaweed that comes in large sheets. You can find kombu in your local Asian supermarket, usually in the Japanese aisle, or you can buy it online.

Chimichurri sauce

This classic sauce goes so well with meat and vegetables you will want to smear it on everything!

90 ml (3 fl oz) water

2 tablespoons apple cider vinegar

22 g (¾ oz/½ cup) finely chopped flat-leaf (Italian) parsley leaves

3 garlic cloves, crushed

1 long red chilli, finely chopped

1 tablespoon dried oregano

½ teaspoon Himalayan salt

½ teaspoon finely ground black pepper

Stir all the ingredients together and taste for flavour, adding more salt and pepper if needed.

TIP The sauce is best served on the day it's made, but can be kept in the fridge in a covered jar or container for 2–3 days.

Happy hot sauce

For those who like things a little hot, this chilli sauce will become your best friend. With no sugar, oils or gluten, this sauce is 100 per cent go!

100 g (3½ oz) long red chillies, tops removed and discarded, chillies roughly chopped

5 garlic cloves, peeled and roughly chopped

4 cm (1½ in) piece of ginger, peeled and roughly chopped

200 ml (7 fl oz) apple cider vinegar

200 ml (7 fl oz) water

2 teaspoons Himalayan salt

Add all the ingredients to a small pot and heat very gently until it just starts to simmer. Allow the pot to gently simmer for 30 minutes.

Allow to cool.

Blend the sauce in a small food processor until very well blended and pour into a clean jar.

Allow the sauce to cool on the bench before, placing a lid on the sauce. Store in the refrigerator for up to 4 weeks.

TIP You can dial the heat up or down depending on your personal preference and this can be achieved by the type of chillies you choose to use in your sauce. I chose long red chillies, which are mild in heat compared to smaller red chillies.

TIP A small message of warning when it comes to chillies. Chilli can inflame the gut in some people so please go carefully when adding any chilli to your food. With this sauce, a little goes a long way.

Ground wakame

Wakame is a dried seaweed much like kombu but has a deeper and more distinct flavour. That being the case, you only need a small pinch to help flavour your food.

1 handful wakame

You will need a small food processor or ideally a spice or coffee grinder for this recipe.

Add the wakame to a processor or spice grinder and blend until fine. The ground wakame should be the same size as table salt, making it perfect for sprinkling and adding flavour to your cooking.

Store the ground wakame in an airtight container in the pantry for up to 3 months.

TIP Buy wakame in a good Asian supermarket in the health food store or order it online.

Spice blends

All my favourite spice blends in one place! Make your own by mixing the spice combinations together and store them for up to 6 months in small airtight containers.

Cowboy spice blend

3 tablespoons ground cumin

3 tablespoons garam masala

1½ tablespoons ground cinnamon

Moroccan spice blend | Ras el hanout

4 teaspoons ground cumin

2 teaspoons Himalayan salt

3 teaspoons black pepper

2 teaspoons ground cinnamon

2 teaspoons ground allspice

2 teaspoons ground coriander

1 teaspoon chilli powder, or to taste

1 teaspoon ground cloves

1 teaspoon nutmeg

1 teaspoon turmeric

Jamaican spice blend

8 teaspoons curry powder

2 teaspoons turmeric

2 teaspoons allspice

pinch to 1 teaspoon chilli powder, or to taste

Garam masala (Indian spice blend)

1 tablespoon curry powder

1 tablespoon ground cumin

2 teaspoons turmeric

2 teaspoons ground coriander

1 teaspoon ground ginger

1 teaspoon ground cardamom

1 teaspoon cinnamon powder

½–1 teaspoon chilli powder, or to taste

Aromatic salt

Give your salt a kick with this fabulously aromatic salt blend.

1 tablespoon fennel seeds

1 tablespoon cumin seeds

½ tablespoon dried rosemary leaves

2 tablespoons ground Himalayan salt

In a frying pan set over medium heat, dry-fry the fennel and cumin seeds for 5 minutes, shaking the seeds often to ensure they don't burn. The smell should be very aromatic.

Add the rosemary leaves and heat for a further 30 seconds, then allow the seeds to cool for 5 minutes.

Add the dry-roasted mixture along with the salt to a small food processor and process on high speed for 30–60 seconds, or until the spices and herb are well blended through the salt.

Store the salt in a small jar and use when you need to add a little flavour!

Roast garlic

Sweet and full of flavour. The simple acting of roasting garlic cloves takes the humble garlic to a whole new taste experience. If you like garlic, but are not keen on garlicky breath, roasting your garlic will take away some of that garlic breath!

1 whole bulb of garlic, separated into single cloves

Preheat the oven to 220°C (425°F). Place the garlic cloves on a piece of foil and wrap like a little parcel.

Place the garlic in the oven and roast for 20 minutes, or until the garlic is soft. Remove from the oven and allow to cool a little before using or storing in the refrigerator for up to 2 weeks.

For the air fryer, preheat the air fryer at 200°C (400°F) for 2 minutes. Add the garlic cloves to the fryer basket. Cook for 5 minutes, then allow to cool a little before using or storing in the refrigerator for up to 2 weeks.

TIP You can oven-roast your garlic or, better still, air-fry them! I have given you methods for both techniques above.

A GUT-FRIENDLY
START TO THE DAY.

This collection of gut-healthy,
filling breakfast recipes is
simple to prepare and budget
friendly, using lots of lean
chicken and turkey, with loads
of flavour - thanks to fresh
herbs and aromatic spices.

As you look through these
recipes, be mindful of how
important it is that we fill our
body with something satisfying
and filling in the morning, so
that we start our day full of
good quality fuel.

A tender chicken patty, my
chicken scotch eggs or prawn
skewers may be as different a
breakfast as you've ever had
but will be the change needed
to get you on the way to good
health and a better life.

Breakfast

Tamari edamame and spiced salt

If you have never thought of having this classic Japanese snack for breakfast, you have been missing out! Naturally gluten-free and high in protein, they are a great early morning snack that can be prepared in advance and eaten on the go.

50 g (1¾ oz) frozen edamame beans (about 18–20 pods)

2 teaspoons low-sodium tamari

pinch of aromatic salt (page 45)

freshly ground black pepper

Defrost your edamame pods by either leaving in a bowl of cold water for 15 minutes, or microwaving on defrost for 4–5 minutes.

Once they are defrosted, heat a small frying pan over medium–high heat and add the edamame pods. Stir to heat through and add the tamari, stirring continuously and cooking for a couple of minutes until the outside of the edamame gets a little charred.

Sprinkle with aromatic salt and pepper and they are ready! To enjoy them at their best, suck on the pod to extract the flavours and suck the soybean from the pod to eat, then discard the pod.

TIP The edamame keep well and can be made up to a week in advance and stored in a covered container in the fridge. They can be eaten warm or cold and if you want to warm them up, pop them in the microwave for 10–20 seconds.

Sticky tofu salad

Whether you are a fan of tofu or not, this mini breakfast salad is a flavour explosion and such a delightful way to start your morning.

50 g (1¾ oz) hard tofu, cut into small dice

1 teaspoon Bridget's sticky sauce (page 25)

1 handful baby basil, mint and coriander (cilantro) leaves

1 lemon or lime wedge, for squeezing

Himalayan salt and freshly ground black pepper

Place the tofu pieces in a small bowl and drizzle over the sticky sauce. Ensure the tofu is well covered in sauce, using fingers to help slosh it on if necessary.

For the air fryer, preheat to 190°C (370°F) for 2 minutes. Lay the tofu pieces in the basket of the fryer in a single layer and cook for 8 minutes.

For a frying pan, heat a small non-stick frying pan over medium heat and add the tofu. Cook the pieces for 4–5 minutes, turning them every minute to ensure they colour on all sides.

Assemble your mini salad by mixing the warm tofu and herbs in a small bowl with a squeeze of lemon and a pinch of salt and pepper.

TIP The best tofu for this simple dish is hard or firm tofu as it fries up nice and crunchy. You can find different types of tofu in any Asian grocery store.

TIP You can use an air fryer to cook your tofu or a frying pan (I have given instructions for both).

Prawn dumplings

I created this recipe for my daughter as a protein-dense breakfast for her and her pescatarian ways. She needed a quick breakfast – grab, dip and go style – and loved the style of yum cha dining, so this delicious slip of a brekkie is perfect for her and anyone who wants the taste without the guilt!

500 g (1 lb 2 oz) raw green prawn (shrimp) tails, frozen or fresh

½ teaspoon low-sodium tamari

4 tablespoons freshly grated ginger

4 tablespoons finely chopped coriander (cilantro) or basil leaves

1 teaspoon Himalayan salt

1 teaspoon finely ground black pepper

tamari and lime dipping sauce, to serve (page 31)

If using frozen prawn tails, defrost for 5 minutes under slow, cold running water. Chop the tails roughly and add to a food processor or blender along with the ½ teaspoon of tamari, grated ginger, coriander or basil leaves, salt and pepper. Pulse a few times to just blend and chop the mixture.

Prepare your pot for steaming, or your steamer equipment as per manufacturer's instructions. If using a pot, add 15 cm (6 in) of warm water to the bottom of a large pot and place the steamer basket on top of the pot. Add a well-fitted lid and set the pot on medium heat and allow the steam to build up in the basket.

Using a set of scales, measure the dumpling mixture with a tablespoon into 25 g (1 oz) balls and let them sit on a piece of non-stick baking paper. You can simplify this task by having a small bowl of cold water next to where you are working. Dip your fingers into the water each time you portion and roll a dumpling.

Once the steam has built up in your steamer, carefully place the dumplings into the basket and steam with the lid on for 3½–4 minutes. Remove the dumplings from the basket and serve with a small dish of the tamari dipping sauce.

TIP I suggest you buy raw (or green) prawns (shrimp). They are so quick and easy to cook yourself and your tastebuds will be forever grateful. Don't fall into the trap of buying precooked prawns, as the flavour is inferior and the prawn meat is so much drier than when you cook them yourself.

Prawn skewers

Prawns for breakfast feels like a treat, but it's a fabulous low-calorie, lean protein example of how good breakfast can be.

70 g (2½ oz) prawn (shrimp) tails, defrosted if frozen (use cold running water)

1 teaspoon very finely chopped coriander (cilantro) stalks

½ teaspoon pure garlic powder

1 teaspoon crushed ginger

1 lemon wedge

pinch of Himalayan salt and freshly ground black pepper

1 teaspoon tamari

½ teaspoon ground wakame (page 40)

oil-free pesto, to serve (page 26)

Place the prawn tails in a small bowl and add the coriander stalks, garlic powder, crushed ginger and the juice from the lemon. Add a pinch of salt and pepper and massage the flavours onto the tails.

Skewer the prawn tails between 2–3 small bamboo skewers.

Heat a small frying pan over medium to high with the tamari and add the skewers. Cook the prawns for 1 minute before flipping and cooking for a further 30–40 seconds.

Remove the skewers from the pan and sprinkle with ground wakame. Serve alongside the oil-free pesto for dipping or drizzling.

TIP I suggest you buy raw (or green) prawns (shrimp). They are quick and easy to cook yourself and your tastebuds will be forever grateful. Don't fall into the trap of buying pre-cooked prawns, as the flavour is inferior and the prawn meat is so much drier than when you cook them yourself.

Chicken breakfast patties

Lean chicken makes for a wonderful breakfast patty, with this particular recipe simply loaded with flavour. Use it as a stand-alone breakfast or as a healthy alternative to sausages and bacon.

1 kg (2 lb 4 oz) skinless chicken breast, roughly chopped

40 g (1½ oz/1 cup) finely chopped coriander (cilantro) leaves and stalks

50 g (1¾ oz/1 cup) finely chopped basil leaves

5 tablespoons grated ginger

4 garlic cloves, crushed

3 teaspoons fine Himalayan salt

2 teaspoons finely ground black pepper

3½ tablespoons Bridget's sticky sauce (page 25)

Place the chicken, coriander, basil, ginger, garlic, salt and black pepper into the bowl of a food processor and pulse until well blended and minced. If you don't have a food processor, use lean minced (ground) chicken and mix everything by hand in a mixing bowl.

Using food scales, line the scales with a bit of baking paper and weigh the chicken mixture into 70 g (21/2 oz) portions. Shape the portions into balls and flatten. Use a small bowl of water to dip your fingers into. This will help you shape the patties.

Heat a large non-stick frying pan over medium–high heat. Spoon 1/2 teaspoon of Bridget's sticky sauce on to the top of four patties. Lay these patties, sticky sauce side down into the hot pan and spoon another 1/2 teaspoon of sticky sauce on the top of the patties. Cook the patties for 2–3 minutes before carefully flipping and cooking for another 2–3 minutes, or until the patty is cooked through.

Alternatively, preheat your air fryer to 180°C (350°F) and place the patties in sticky sauce in the air fryer for 8–10 minutes, or until cooked through.

Remove from the air fryer or pan to cool and continue cooking the patties with sticky sauce in batches until they are all done.

The patties will keep in the refrigerator for up to 4 days or vacuum sealed for up to 2 weeks. They can be also be frozen for 3 months and defrosted in the bottom of the fridge overnight. To reheat, microwave for 20–30 seconds.

TIP You can use lean minced turkey as a substitute for the chicken.

Yum cha-style breakfast chicken dumplings

Who doesn't love yum cha? That wonderful Cantonese style of dining that involves small plates of tasty and delicious steamed parcels of goodness. This recipe takes the yum cha model and turns it a little on its head in the most delectable way!

500 g (1 lb 2 oz) skinless chicken breast, roughly chopped

3 tablespoons roughly chopped coriander (cilantro), including stalks

2 tablespoons roughly chopped flat-leaf (Italian) parsley

1 tablespoon finely chopped chives

1 tablespoon crushed garlic

2 teaspoons crushed ginger

2 teaspoons Chinese five-spice

1 teaspoon ground coriander

1½ teaspoons Himalayan salt

1 teaspoon freshly ground black pepper

1 tablespoon low-sodium tamari

tamari and lime dipping sauce, to serve (page 31)

Prepare the pot for steaming, or your steamer equipment as per manufacturer's instructions. If using a pot, add 15 cm (6 in) of warm water to the bottom of a large pot and place the steamer basket on top of the pot. Add a well-fitted lid and set the pot on medium heat and allow the steam to build up in the basket.

Make the dumplings by adding all the ingredients, except the tamari sauce, to a food processor and process for 10–15 seconds or until the chicken is in small pieces and the ingredients are well blended. Don't let the meat get too fine, or your dumplings will come out hard.

Using a set of scales, measure the dumpling mixture into 25 g (1 oz) balls and let them sit on a piece of non-stick baking paper. You can simplify this task by having a small bowl of cold water next to where you are working. Dip your fingers into the water each time you portion and roll a dumpling.

Once the steam has built up in your steamer, carefully place the dumplings into the basket and steam with the lid on for 4 minutes. Remove the dumplings from the basket and serve with a small dish of the tamari and lime sauce for dipping.

TIP I like to mince my own chicken as I make sure that the meat is as lean as possible by only using the breast. I also find that pro-cessed minced (ground) chicken is too fine and the dumplings come out tough. Thicker mince is ideal for this recipe! You can swap turkey for chicken in this recipe as well.

Chicken gravy quiche

A crustless chicken quiche is just the thing we need to grab and go for a quick breakfast when you're running out the door. Make these little beauties in advance and store them in the fridge.

3 tablespoons Bridget's sticky sauce (page 25)

420 g (15 oz) raw chicken breast, thinly sliced

2 teaspoons finely chopped garlic

2 teaspoons finely chopped ginger

2 tablespoons kombu water (page 34)

6 eggs

4 tablespoons finely chopped flat-leaf (Italian) parsley, coriander (cilantro) or chives

Himalayan salt and freshly ground black pepper

Preheat the oven to 180°C (350°F). Heat a heavy-based frying pan over medium–high heat and add the sticky sauce and chicken breast. Stir to combine and add the garlic and ginger. Stir and cook the chicken for a couple of minutes until just cooked through.

Remove the chicken from the pan and set aside to cool a little. Add the kombu water to the pan and create a little gravy by using a spatula to scrape the base of the pan to extract all the flavours. Remove the pan from the heat.

When the chicken is cool enough to handle, shred the meat and season with a little salt and pepper.

Place 6 muffin cases into the muffin tray holes and crack an egg into each case. Lightly whisk the egg with a fork and distribute the chopped herbs evenly through the muffin cases.

Using a set of scales to assist you, evenly portion out the cooked chicken and add each portion to the muffin cases and stir through. Finish each quiche with a spoon of the gravy and stir through.

Place the muffin tray into the oven and bake for 15–18 minutes, or until the quiches are cooked through. Remove from the oven and allow the quiches to cool on a wire rack. Store for up to 1 week in the refrigerator.

TIP You will need a deep muffin tray, also known as Texas muffin tray, to make these quiches and large paper or foil muffin cases.

Chicken and herb breakfast salad

Throw caution to the proverbial wind and eat a tasty little chicken salad for breakfast. You can either use up leftover roast chicken or cook off a bit of fresh tasty minced (ground) chicken. Either way it's a fabulous way to say good morning to your tastebuds! The protein helps you stay fuller longer and it sure beats having a piece of toast or a muffin!

1 handful baby basil, mint and coriander (cilantro) leaves

Minced chicken filling

1 tablespoon low-sodium tamari, plus 1 teaspoon extra

70 g (½ oz) lean minced (ground) chicken

1 garlic clove, crushed

½ teaspoon crushed ginger

Himalayan salt and freshly ground pepper, to taste

1 teaspoon ground cumin

1 teaspoon ground coriander

2 teaspoons freshly chopped coriander (cilantro) stalks

4 tablespoons water

OR

60 g (2¼ oz) shredded roast chicken (breast preferably, skin removed)

½ tablespoon Bridget's sticky sauce (page 25)

If using the minced (ground) chicken option in this recipe, heat a large frying pan over medium–high heat with a teaspoon of tamari. Quickly add the garlic and ginger and stir-fry for 30 seconds. Add the chicken and, using a wooden spoon, break up the chicken into small pieces. Season well with salt and pepper.

Allow the chicken to cook for 5 minutes, stirring frequently, then add the cumin and coriander powders along with the chopped coriander stalks. Stir in well.

Stir the remaining 1 tablespoon of tamari into the water and add the liquid to the chicken. (At this stage it may look like you are making mince soup, but don't be concerned. As the liquid reduces down it creates a wonderfully tasty gravy!)

Cook the liquid down for about 5 minutes, or until it has formed a thick gravy. Taste for flavour, adding more salt and pepper to taste. Remove from the heat and keep warm.

If you are using shredded cooked chicken, ensure the sticky sauce has coated the chicken pieces.

Combine your salad by adding the chicken to the fresh herb leaves. Season with a little salt and pepper and toss through the herb leaves. Serve immediately.

Jamaican-spiced chicken skewers

This Jamaican-style dry rub is perfect for chicken and works well whether you are making these delicious skewers or turning the chicken into a fabulous curry.

2 limes, juiced

350 g (12 oz) chicken breast, skin removed and cut into bite-sized chunks

3 teaspoons curry powder

½ teaspoon turmeric

1 teaspoon allspice

Himalayan salt and freshly ground black pepper

2 lime or lemon wedges, to serve

tamari and lime dipping sauce, to serve (page 31)

Marinate the chicken pieces in a small bowl by pouring over the lime juice and mixing well. Sprinkle over the curry powder, turmeric and allspice and season with a little salt and pepper. Stir the chicken and spices until they are well covered and evenly distributed.

At this stage you can leave the chicken in the refrigerator to marinate overnight. This will help to develop the flavours. If you are pushed for time, move on to the next step.

Weigh the chicken pieces into 35 g (1¼ oz) portions. You will get 10 small piles of chicken pieces. Using 6-inch bamboo skewers, thread the 35 g (1¼ oz) lots onto 10 skewers.

Heat a large frying pan, sandwich press or barbecue to high and add the skewers, cooking in batches if necessary. In my sandwich press, the skewers take 2–3 minutes, but you may need a little longer depending on what you are using. The secret to a delicious skewer is not to overcook the chicken. Remove the skewers when the chicken is just cooked.

Serve sprinkled with a little salt and pepper, lemon wedges for squeezing and a side of the tamari sauce for dipping.

TIP I cook these skewers in my sandwich press on high. It's non-stick and takes about 3 minutes to cook, plus it's so easy to clean. If you can easily heat up the barbecue, do so! These skewers are wonderful cooked on a barbecue.

Chicken scotch eggs

I first tried a scotch egg in the home of the fabled egg, England. I discovered that the egg got its name from the mincing of the meat that covers the egg, which is referred to as scotching. You will need an air fryer for this recipe.

1 teaspoon bicarbonate of soda (baking soda)

7 eggs

490 g (1 lb 1 oz) chicken breast, roughly chopped

1 green apple, peeled, cored and diced (optional)

2 teaspoons chopped ginger

2 teaspoons chopped garlic

1 small handful coriander (cilantro) leaves

1 small handful flat-leaf (Italian) parsley leaves

1 tablespoon Bridget's sticky sauce, plus 7 teaspoons extra (page 25)

Himalayan salt and freshly ground black pepper

Bring a pot of water to the boil along with the bicarbonate of soda. Using a large spoon, carefully lower the eggs into the boiling water. For soft-boiled eggs, boil for 4½ minutes. For semi-hard, boil for 5½ minutes and for hard-boiled, boil for 6½ minutes.

Remove the pot immediately from the heat and run the pot under cold water to stop the eggs from cooking. As soon as you can pick the egg up, carefully roll the egg on the bench to crack the shell which will help the egg to cool down more quickly. Set the eggs aside to cool while you prepare the chicken mixture.

Place the chicken breast, apple if using, ginger, garlic, herbs and 1 tablespoon of sticky sauce into the bowl of a blender or food processor. Season with a little salt and pepper and blend on high until very well combined.

Using scales, divide the chicken mixture into 7 portions.

Very carefully continue to peel the eggs, making sure not to split the eggs. Take your time with the peeling in order to do it correctly.

Take a portion of the chicken and flatten it as much as possible in the palm of a your hand. Sit the egg on top of the chicken and bring the chicken up to cover the egg as evenly as possible. This may take a little practice to get right, so take your time.

Once all the eggs are covered, preheat your air fryer for 2 minutes to 180°C (350°F). Add the rest of the sticky sauce to a bowl and roll the scotch eggs in the sauce to fully cover the outside of the eggs.

Place the eggs inside the air fryer basket and cook for 7–8 minutes until well covered and the chicken is fully cooked. Cool the eggs before storing in the fridge.

TIP You can make these in advance. They will last 4 days in the fridge or you can vacuum seal them and increase their fridge shelf life up to 2 weeks.

Sticky chicken

It's not just the name that renders me weak at the knees but the look and taste of this great technique for cooking chicken is wonderful in every single way. As the name suggests, the chicken has a sticky glaze and is wonderfully tender and moist.

500 g (1 lb 2 oz) chicken breast, sliced into thin, even strips like a tenderloin

5 tablespoons Bridget's sticky sauce (page 25)

Himalayan salt and freshly ground black pepper

If using an oven, preheat the oven to 200°C (400°F) and line a small roasting dish with non-stick baking paper.

For the air fryer, set to 200°C (400°F) and preheat for 2 minutes.

Lay the sliced chicken onto a plate and pour over the sticky sauce. Using your hands, massage the sticky sauce over the chicken, ensuring all the chicken is well covered in sauce.

Lay the chicken into the basket of the air fryer, ensuring the chicken is in a single layer. Depending on the size of your air fryer, you may have to cook the chicken in batches.

Cook the chicken for 8–10 minutes, or until cooked through but still moist! Season with a little salt and pepper before serving with your desired accompaniment.

For the oven-baked sticky chicken, place the chicken strips onto the roasting dish in a single layer and bake in the oven for 9–12 minutes or until cooked through but still moist. Season with a little salt and pepper before serving.

TIP I use an air fryer to make my sticky chicken but I have also provided the method for oven cooking. The oven method, although still delicious, does not colour up as well as the air fryer version.

Turkey meatballs

These meatballs are so full of flavour. The herbs complement the lean minced (ground) turkey so well and they are a wonderful alternative to chicken breakfast patties!

500 g (1 lb 2 oz) lean minced (ground) turkey

3 garlic cloves, crushed

2 tablespoons grated ginger

4 teaspoons fresh or dried rosemary

2 teaspoons fresh or dry thyme leaves

2 teaspoons chopped coriander (cilantro) stalks

2 teaspoons tamari, plus 1 tablespoon extra

2 teaspoons Himalayan salt

2 teaspoons freshly ground black pepper

Make the meatballs by mixing together the turkey, garlic, ginger, rosemary, thyme, coriander stalks and tamari. Add the salt and pepper and stir through.

Roll the meatballs into 14 equal-sized balls approximately 35 g (1¼ oz) in weight.

Heat a large frying pan over medium heat with 1 tablespoon of tamari, or preheat the air fryer to 200°C (400°F) for 2 minutes

Add the meatballs to the pan and cook the balls for 5–8 minutes, rolling them often to ensure they cook evenly.

Depending on the size of your pan, you may have to work in batches to cook all the meatballs, adding another tablespoon of tamari if needed.

If using the air fryer, add the meatballs to the fryer basket and cook for 7–8 minutes.

Remove the meatballs from the heat and serve. If storing, allow to cool completely before storing in a covered container in the fridge. These meatballs will last 4–5 days if stored correctly.

TIP You can use a frying pan or air fryer to cook the meatballs. I have given you the method for both.

Chicken egg foo yong with gravy

Breakfast just got better with my chicken egg foo yong complete with a flavoursome pour-over gravy!

2 tablespoons Bridget's sticky sauce (page 25)

140 g (5 oz) chicken breast, thinly sliced

1 teaspoon finely chopped garlic

1 teaspoon finely chopped ginger

½ teaspoon Chinese five-spice

½ teaspoon cumin powder

60 ml (2 fl oz/¼ cup) kombu water (page 34)

1 tablespoon inulin powder

Himalayan salt and freshly ground black pepper

2 large eggs

1 tablespoon finely chopped flat-leaf (Italian) parsley leaves

1 tablespoon finely chopped coriander (cilantro) stalks or chives

1 small handful herb leaves such as mint, parsley or coriander (cilantro), to serve

Heat a heavy-based frying pan over medium–high heat and add the sticky sauce followed quickly by the sliced chicken. Stir-fry for a few seconds, then add the garlic, ginger, five-spice and cumin powders. Stir-fry for a further 2–3 minutes, or until the chicken is just cooked through.

Remove the chicken from the pan and place the pan back over medium heat. Add the kombu water, inulin powder and a sprinkling of salt and pepper. Bubble the liquid for a minute or so until the gravy thickens a little. Taste for flavour, adding a little more ginger or garlic if you think it needs it. Pour the gravy into a little jug or bowl and set aside.

Whisk the eggs in a bowl and add the chopped herbs. Shred the chicken and add to the eggs, along with a little salt and pepper, and whisk well to combine.

Clean the frying pan and place back over medium heat. Lay a piece of non-stick baking paper into to base of the pan large enough so that the paper comes up the sides.

Pour the egg mixture into the pan and allow to cook for 3–4 minutes before adding the lid and allowing the egg to cook through for a further 3–4 minutes until fully cooked. As the egg cooks, keep an eye on it, making sure that the base isn't getting too dark. Turn the heat down a little if you think it's cooking too fast and browning too deeply.

Remove the egg foo yong from the pan and peel off the baking paper. Fold the egg in half or thirds and slice down the middle to get two portions, and serve with herbs on top and gravy on the side.

THE HERO THAT IS LUNCHTIME.

It is often with bated breath that I count down the time to when lunch can be enjoyed so I have made quite the fuss, giving you as many lunchtime recipe options as possible.

From tender beef soaked in my famous sticky sauce, right through to a collection of slightly pickled vegetables and moist pulled chicken, there are so many wonderful ways that we can eat delicious food whilst maintaining a healthy diet.

Remembering that these recipes are a guideline, feel free to swap chicken for turkey and broccoli for cauliflower. Eat seasonal wherever you can, which will not only help keep the budget in check but will also mean you are eating food when it's at its best.

Lunch

Spiced beef in cucumber boats

The spiced beef is the hero of this dish. Well-flavoured and tasty, it partners extremely well with a crunchy cucumber. Don't be afraid to chop up the herbs and lay them on top for a wonderful addition in flavour.

1 teaspoon low-sodium tamari

100 g (3½ oz) lean minced (ground) beef

2 garlic cloves, peeled and crushed

1 teaspoon finely grated ginger

2 heaped teaspoons cowboy spice (page 42)

3 tablespoons tamari and lime sauce (page 31)

Himalayan salt and freshly ground black pepper

300 g (10½ oz) Lebanese (short) cucumbers

1 small handful coriander (cilantro), basil or mint leaves, finely chopped

Heat a large non-stick frying pan over medium–high temperature with the tamari and break in the beef. Stirring well with a wooden spoon, continue to break up the beef as it cooks and browns for about 5 minutes.

Add the garlic and ginger and stir well to combine. Allow the beef to cook for a further 5–10 minutes, stirring often until the beef is well cooked, browned and dry.

Turn the heat down to medium and add 2 heaped tablespoons of the cowboy spice blend and stir through. Add 3 tablespoons of the tamari and lime sauce and stir through. Taste the beef for flavour, adding salt and pepper to taste.

Cut the cucumbers in half lengthways and using a teaspoon, scrape out some of the seeds to form a little hollow in the cucumber and discard the seeds. Add the beef to your cucumber boats and top with your chopped herbs and a grinding of salt and pepper.

TIP Swap out the meat. Instead of beef, you can use firm tofu, or minced (ground) lamb, chicken or turkey.

Lamb and broccolini stir-fry

The simplicity of this dish is heightened with the addition of one of my favourite spice combinations – cowboy spice.

1 teaspoon low-sodium tamari

50 g (1¾ oz) onion, finely diced

2 teaspoons grated ginger

1 garlic clove, crushed

½ green chilli, finely diced (optional)

100 g (3½ oz) lean lamb mince (ground)

3 teaspoons cowboy spice blend (page 42)

1 tablespoon Bridget's sticky sauce (page 25)

4 tablespoons water

Himalayan salt and freshly ground black pepper

140 g (5 oz) broccolini, ends cut off and discarded, chopped in half

2 tablespoons finely chopped mint

2 tablespoons finely chopped coriander (cilantro)

Heat a large frying pan or wok over medium heat with the tamari and add the onions, ginger and garlic. Stir-fry for a couple of minutes, then add the chilli along with the lamb mince.

Turn the heat up a little and add the cowboy spice and sticky sauce and stir-fry the mixture for 2–3 minutes, or until cooked through. Add the water and season well with salt and pepper and turn the heat back down to medium. Allow the mixture to bubble gently for 3–4 minutes so that the flavour of the meat goes throughout the liquid.

Pour the contents of the pan into a bowl and place the pan back on the heat. Add the broccolini to the pan and enough water so that the water only covers the broccolini halfway. Turn the heat up to high and allow the broccolini to steam and simmer for about 2 minutes until just cooked through, so it's tender but still firm to the bite.

Drain all the water from the pan, place the pan back over medium heat and add the lamb and liquid back into the pan. Stir to combine. Season with a little salt and pepper and spoon onto a serving plate. Sprinkle with the fresh herbs and serve.

Cucumber and beef sam'ich

If you had asked me a few weeks ago whether I would enjoy eating a whole cucumber like a sandwich, I would have told you "You're dreaming mate!" But after partaking of a lunch filled with these incredible delights, I am now hooked and patiently waiting for lunchtime so I can go another sam'ich round.

300 g (10½ oz) Lebanese (short) cucumbers

85 g (3 oz) cooked beef, either roasted and thinly sliced, or seared and thinly sliced

3 teaspoons oil-free pesto (page 26)

3 teaspoons sugar-free dijon mustard (optional)

1 handful small basil leaves

Himalayan salt and freshly ground black pepper

Peel the cucumbers and cut the tips off each end. Cut the cucumbers in half lengthways and using a teaspoon, scrape out some of the seeds to create a little hollow in each cucumber.

Spoon 1 teaspoon of the oil-free pesto along one hollow, and if using, lay 1 teaspoon of mustard along the other. Distribute and layer the beef slices along the pesto-lined cucumbers and top the beef with some of the basil leaves.

Season well with salt and pepper and top the sam'ich with the other half of the cucumber. Feel free to sprinkle the whole sam'ich with a little more salt. Repeat until you have made up all the cucumbers.

TIP Choose a small firm cucumber, like a Lebanese (short) cucumber. They are much easier to eat and have a lovely texture.

TIP The use of mustard here is totally optional. I am a mustard LOVER so any chance I can get, I like to smear it on. I choose Maille dijon mustard as it has no added sugar or nasties.

Cottage pie – beef mince and roasted garlic cauliflower mash

This tasty filling is such a wonderful base for the super-creamy roast garlic cauliflower mash.

Cauliflower mash

5 garlic cloves, skin on

340 g (11¾ oz) cauliflower florets

Himalayan salt and freshly ground black pepper

2 teaspoons finely chopped rosemary leaves

pinch of nutmeg

pinch of cumin

Beef and onion filling

3 tablespoons tamari, plus 1 teaspoon extra

1 onion, finely chopped

3 garlic cloves, crushed

200 g (7 oz) lean minced (ground) beef

1 tablespoon ground cumin

1 tablespoon ground coriander

2 teaspoons finely chopped rosemary leaves

200 ml (7 fl oz) water

Preheat the oven to 220°C (425°F). Place the garlic cloves on a piece of foil and wrap like a little parcel. Place the garlic in the oven and roast for 20 minutes, or until soft. Remove from the oven and set aside.

Place the cauliflower florets in a pot with just enough water to cover and season with a teaspoon of salt. Bring the water to the boil, then reduce the heat until the water is rapidly simmering. Cook the cauliflower for 12–15 minutes, or until very tender. Drain the cooked cauliflower and keep warm in the pot with a lid on it.

Cook the beef by heating a large frying pan over medium–high heat with 1 teaspoon of tamari. Quickly add the onions and raw garlic and stir-fry for 2–3 minutes. Add the beef and using a wooden spoon, break up the beef into small pieces. Season well with salt and pepper.

Allow the beef to cook for 5 minutes, stirring frequently, then add the cumin and coriander powders with the chopped rosemary. Stir in well.

Stir the remaining 3 tablespoons of tamari into the water and add the liquid to the beef. Cook the liquid down for about 10 minutes, or until it has formed a thick gravy. Taste for flavour, adding salt and pepper to taste. Remove the pan from the heat and keep warm.

Finish off the cauliflower mash by placing the cooked florets into a small blender along with the flesh squeezed from the roasted garlic cloves. Season with salt and pepper and add the rosemary leaves along with the nutmeg and cumin. Blend until very smooth.

Place the warm beef in the base of a small pie dish or bowl and top with the smooth cauliflower mash. Serve warm.

Slow cooked lamb and garlic stew with broccoli

A lean cut of lamb benefits greatly from a slow cook, becoming tender and delicious. This lamb is wonderful to leave on overnight if you have a slow cooker, or a fabulous weekend project to slow braise gently throughout the day.

2 teaspoons low-sodium tamari

200 g (7 oz) lean lamb shoulder or lamb leg, fat trimmed and cut into cubes

100 g (3½ oz) onion, peeled and cut into chunky dice

20 garlic cloves, peeled

3 slices fresh ginger

1 teaspoon ground ginger powder

3 tablespoons Moroccan spice blend (page 42)

600 ml (21 fl oz) kombu water and kombu pieces (page 34)

2 stalks of fresh rosemary

Himalayan salt and pepper

280 g (10 oz) broccoli florets

2 lemon wedges, to serve

1 handful mint leaves, to serve

Heat a casserole dish, Dutch oven or large frying pan over medium to high heat and add the tamari sauce and lamb. Stir and brown the lamb cubes for a couple of minutes and then add the onion, garlic cloves and ginger slices. Fry for a further couple of minutes, stirring occasionally, then add the ginger powder and Moroccan spice blend and fry for 30 seconds.

Add the kombu water, kombu pieces and rosemary stalks and season well with salt and pepper. If using a slow cooker, add the contents of the pan to the slow cooker and cook on low overnight for 8 hours, or until the lamb is perfectly tender.

If using a casserole dish or Dutch oven, preheat the oven to 120°C (235°F). Place the lid on the casserole and place the dish in the oven and bake slowly for 4–6 hours, or until the lamb is tender.

When the lamb is ready and incredibly tender, plunge the broccoli florets into boiling water for 1 minute. Drain the broccoli before adding to the slow-cooked lamb. Stir the broccoli through the lamb and taste the stew for flavour, adding more salt and pepper to taste.

Serve with a wedge of lemon and a handful of mint leaves.

Korean-style beef with pickled cucumbers and basil

If you have ever been to a Korean barbecue, then you know how incredible it is. The aroma that wafts from the sizzling meat is wonderfully intoxicating and deliciously flavoured. Combined with the vinegary taste of pickle, it is a pleasure to behold. In this recipe I have used a Korean-style barbecue sauce, aptly named "sticky sauce" that helps marinate the beef before it gets a quick frizzle in a hot pan. Once you have made your pickles and sticky sauce, this is a 5-minute dish to make.

100 g (3½ oz) lean beef, thinly sliced and slightly flattened

1½ tablespoons Bridget's sticky sauce (page 25)

150 g (5½ oz) pickled cucumbers (page 246)

150 g (5½ oz) cucumber, thinly sliced

1 small handful basil leaves

Himalayan salt and freshly ground black pepper

Cover the beef slices with the sticky sauce and massage it into the meat. If you have time, marinate the beef overnight to allow the flavours to develop.

When ready to cook, heat a small frying pan over high heat and add the beef slices, cooking quickly for about 1 minute or until the beef is just cooked through and the smell coming from your pan is intoxicating!

Remove the beef from the pan and plate up immediately with a mixture of the pickled and fresh cucumbers, some basil and a good sprinkling of salt and pepper.

TIP Use lean beef and for an added flavour dimension, marinate the beef slices in the sticky sauce overnight.

TIP I use a combination of pickled and fresh cucumbers to mix it up and increase the flavour, but it's up to you whether you use fresh or pickled or, like me, a combination of the two.

Healthy steak 'n' onions on mash

I grew up longing for breakfast at my grandma's house, because breakfast usually meant a huge tray of steak, onions and gravy, and a big pot of creamy mashed potatoes. One of the hardest parts about being on a diet is not being able to eat some of the food you associate with love and happy memories, so it is with such thoughts in mind that I thought we all needed a plate of healthy steak, onions and gravy with a creamy mash.

Cauliflower mash

3 garlic cloves, skin on

170 g (6 oz) cauliflower florets

Himalayan salt and freshly ground black pepper

1 teaspoon finely chopped thyme leaves

pinch of nutmeg

pinch of cumin

70 g (2½ oz) red onion, thinly sliced

2 tablespoons low-sodium tamari

100 g (3½ oz) piece of lean beef, like fillet or rump

1 teaspoon thyme leaves

Preheat the oven to 220°C (425°F) and place the garlic cloves on a piece of foil and wrap like a parcel. Place the garlic in the oven and roast for 20 minutes, or until the garlic is soft. Remove from the oven and set aside.

Place the cauliflower florets in a pot with just enough water to cover and season with a teaspoon of salt. Bring the water to the boil, then reduce the heat until the water is rapidly simmering. Cook the cauliflower for 12–15 minutes, or until very tender.

Drain the water from the cooked cauliflower and mash by placing the cooked florets into a small powerful blender along with the flesh squeezed from the roasted garlic cloves. Season with salt and pepper and add the rosemary leaves along with the nutmeg and cumin. Blend until very smooth. Place some foil over the mash to keep warm while you prepare the remaining ingredients.

Heat a heavy-based frying pan over medium–hot temperature and when there is a light haze coming off the pan, add the onions and 1 tablespoon of tamari. Cook the onions for 3–5 minutes, stirring frequently until the onions are soft and tender. Remove from the pan and set aside.

continued overleaf

Healthy steak 'n' onions on mash

With the pan back over medium—high heat, wait for the light haze to come off the pan again and then add the steak. Season the steak with salt and pepper and cook the steak for 1 minute, before flipping and cooking on the other side for 1 minute. Remove the steak from the pan, and allow it to rest with the onions under a little foil.

Add 1 more tablespoon of tamari to the pan together with 3 tablespoons of water and create a little gravy in the pan, swirling and stirring with a wooden spoon to pick up any flavours that may have cooked on to the bottom of the pan. Toss in a few sprigs of thyme leaves and season with a little salt and pepper.

Serve the cauliflower mash on the plate topped with the steak and scattered with the cooked onions. Finish with a drizzle of the pan gravy.

TIP Choose a lean cut for your portion of steak. I like to use a fillet steak, as it's extremely lean and super tasty but you can also use a thin slice of rump, which is lean and flavoursome too.

TIP If raw garlic isn't your thing, roasted garlic will be your best friend! When garlic is roasted in a hot oven, whole in its skins, the flavour mellows and sweetens making it a wonderful addition to soups, dressings and dishes like cauliflower mash.

Broccoli pesto rice bowl with lamb and onion

A wonderful alternative to a rice bowl is my pesto-flavoured broccoli rice bowl with flavoursome lamb and fresh herbs. Enjoy this low-carb fiesta!

140 g (5 oz) broccoli florets

1 tablespoon oil-free pesto (page 26)

1 teaspoon low-sodium tamari

2 teaspoons freshly grated ginger

1 garlic clove, crushed

½ green chilli, finely diced (optional)

100 g (3½ oz) lean lamb, finely sliced

3 teaspoons cowboy spice blend (page 42)

1 tablespoon Bridget's sticky sauce (page 25)

4 tablespoons water

Himalayan salt and freshly ground black pepper

50 g (1¾ oz) red onion, very thinly sliced

1 teaspoon cumin seeds

1 small handful basil and mint leaves

lemon wedge, to serve

Cut the broccoli florets into small pieces and add them to a food processor. Blend the broccoli for 20–30 seconds, or until it resembles rice.

At this stage you can store your broccoli rice in the fridge for up to 3 days, or you can freeze it in zip lock bags in the freezer for up to 2 months.

Heat a frying pan or wok over medium heat with the tamari. Add the ginger and garlic and stir-fry for a couple of minutes. Add the chilli along with the lamb, and stir fry for a minute.

Turn the heat up a little and add the cowboy spice and sticky sauce. Stir-fry the mixture for 1 minute, or until cooked through. Add the water and season well with salt and pepper. Reduce the heat to medium and allow the mixture to bubble gently for 2 minutes so that the flavour of the meat goes throughout the liquid.

To cook your broccoli rice, cover with plastic wrap and microwave on high for 3 minutes. Season well with salt and pepper and stir through the oil-free pesto.

Plate up by placing the broccoli rice in the bowl followed by the lamb and sauce. Top with the sliced red onions, herbs, cumin seeds and a sprinkling of salt and pepper. Serve with the lemon wedge.

Quick beef and zucchini stir-fry

Lunch in 10 minutes … what could be better than that? This dish ticks so many boxes. It's quick, it's delicious, it's fresh and it's fuss free. This is my ideal lunch.

1 tablespoon Bridget's sticky sauce (page 25)

100 g (3½ oz) lean beef, thinly sliced

Himalayan salt and freshly ground black pepper

200 g (7 oz) zucchini (courgette), sliced into ribbons

100 ml (3½ fl oz) kombu water (page 34)

2 tablespoons chopped coriander (cilantro)

Heat a large non-stick wok or frying pan over medium–high heat and add the sticky sauce. Add the beef and stir-fry for 60–90 seconds, or until the beef is cooked through.

Remove the beef from the pan and season with salt and pepper.

Place the pan or wok back on the heat and add the zucchini. Stir-fry for 30 seconds, then add the kombu water and season with salt and pepper. Stir-fry the zucchini for a further 30 seconds, then remove from the heat.

Toss through the cooked beef and chopped herbs and serve!

TIP I use a mandolin slicer or rex peeler (page 19) to create the zucchini ribbons as it's much easier and much more effective than peeling them by hand.

TIP If you don't like coriander don't worry, you are not alone! You can swap the coriander with mint, basil or chives.

Fast or slow cooked beef pot roast

Imagine a fall-apart piece of beef and you get the idea of why this dish is wonderful. Nestled in a succulent stew, this dish will warm the belly and the heart! You can choose to slow cook it or speed up the process and use a pressure cooker like I have. The choice is yours as the results are fabulous using either method.

120 ml (4 fl oz) kombu water (page 34)

90 ml (3 fl oz) low-sodium tamari

120 ml (4 fl oz) strong black brewed coffee

8 garlic cloves, finely chopped

3 tablespoons freshly grated ginger

2 onions, peeled and diced

1.5 kg (3 lb 5 oz) beef chuck, blade or round steak, diced into large pieces

1 tablespoon freshly ground black pepper

2 portions cauliflower mash (page 260)

Whisk together the kombu water with the tamari, coffee, garlic and ginger.

Place the onions and beef into the bowl of your pressure cooker or slow cooker, pour over the liquid mixture and add the pepper. Stir to combine.

If using a pressure cooker, cook on medium–high for 1 hour. If using a slow cooker, cook the pot roast on high for 6–8 hours, or until tender (or as per manufacturer's instructions for cooking a pot roast).

If using a heavy-bottomed pot, cook on low for 6–8 hours, stirring occasionally to make sure the meat doesn't stick to the bottom of the pot.

When the meat is tender, check the sauce for flavour, adding more tamari or pepper if necessary. If the sauce seems a little watery, you can bring the pot roast to the boil and allow it to reduce in volume until the sauce thickens to your liking.

Serve this pot roast on top of warm cauliflower mash and sprinkle over a few fresh herbs like parsley or basil for added flavour before serving.

TIP I made my pot roast using a pressure cooker and it took just over an hour. You can also use a slow cooker set on high overnight, or you can slowly cook it in a pot set on low on the stove for 6–8 hours.

Lamb cutlets with onion jam and curried cauliflower

This is one of my favourite dishes as it combines all the flavours that I love. The lamb is tender, the cauliflower purée is fragrant and the sweetness from the cooked onions brings everything together for a fabulous lunch.

1 teaspoon low-sodium tamari

140 g (5 oz) red onion, thinly sliced

100 ml (¾ fl oz) kombu water (page 34)

1 teaspoon finely chopped thyme leaves

Himalayan salt and freshly ground black pepper

340 g (11¾ oz) cauliflower florets, chopped into small pieces

200 g (7 oz) lamb cutlets, trimmed of any visible fat

2 tablespoons oil-free pesto (page 26)

3 roasted garlic cloves, mashed (page 46)

2 teaspoons curry powder

1 teaspoon garam masala

1 teaspoon turmeric

1 small handful mint leaves

Preheat the oven grill (broiler) to high and place a wire rack on a roasting tray.

Heat a small frying pan over medium heat and add the tamari and the red onion. Sauté for a few minutes, then add the kombu broth and thyme leaves. Reduce the heat to medium–low and cook the onions for 20 minutes, stirring often to prevent them catching and burning.

Place the cauliflower in a small pot, just cover with water and add a pinch of salt. Bring to the boil, then cook for 12–15 minutes or until the cauliflower is very tender.

Meanwhile, cover the lamb cutlets with the pesto and season well with salt and pepper. Place them on the wire rack and cook under the grill and cook for 7–8 minutes, turning once. You could also place the cutlets in an air fryer set to 200°C (400°F) and cook for 5–7 minutes.

Drain the water from the cauliflower, making sure to shake the cauliflower as it drains to get as much water off as possible. Add the garlic, curry powder, garam masala and turmeric to the cauliflower and blend with a small food processor or stick blender until well puréed. Taste for flavour and season with salt and pepper.

Serve the cutlets with a side of the curried mash, some of the onions and a sprinkling of the mint leaves.

TIP When weighing your lamb, remember not to weigh the bone, just the meat!

Barbecued sticky beef skewers on cucumber salad

The simple combination of my sticky sauce and lean beef cooked over charcoal produces a glorious dish.

100 g (3½ oz) lean beef rump or porterhouse, diced into cubes

2 tablespoons Bridget's sticky sauce (page 25)

1 tablespoon apple cider vinegar

1 teaspoon inulin powder

Himalayan salt and freshly ground black pepper

300 g (10½ oz) cucumber, sliced

1 tablespoon finely chopped mint leaves, basil leaves, dill or coriander (cilantro)

Add the diced beef to a small bowl and drizzle over 1 tablespoon of the sticky sauce. Massage the sticky sauce into the beef with your fingers and cover the bowl with plastic wrap. Marinate overnight or for at least 2 hours.

When ready to cook, place the skewers onto a hot barbecue, under a hot grill (broiler) or in a sandwich press and cook for 4–8 minutes or until the beef is cooked through.

While the beef cooks, make the salad dressing by stirring together the vinegar and inulin with a pinch of salt. Pour the dressing over the sliced cucumber and sprinkle with the fresh herbs and a grinding of black pepper.

Serve the skewers on top of the salad.

TIP Ideally, marinate the beef overnight in the sticky sauce for maximum flavour effect!

TIP Inulin powder is a soluble fibre and derived from chicory root. Inulin is a prebiotic so it helps improve gut health, can help relieve constipation, helps to curb your appetite and it's 100% natural. It also has a slight sweetness to it, making it very user friendly! You can find inulin powder at your health food store or search for it online.

TIP These skewers can be cooked ahead of time and stored in the fridge for up to 2 days, or in the freezer for 1 month.

Curried shepherd's pie

The classic shepherd's pie gets a healthy flavour upgrade thanks to fragrant spices and a tasty creamy cauliflower mash.

Cauliflower mash

5 garlic cloves, skin on

340 g (11¾ oz) raw cauliflower florets

Himalayan salt and freshly ground black pepper

2 teaspoons finely chopped rosemary leaves

pinch of nutmeg

pinch of cumin

Curried lamb and onion filling

3 tablespoons low-sodium tamari, plus 1 teaspoon extra

1 onion, finely chopped

2 teaspoons finely chopped garlic

200 g (7 oz) lean minced (ground) lamb

1 tablespoon ground cumin

1 tablespoon ground coriander

2 teaspoons curry powder

1 teaspoon turmeric

300 ml (10½ fl oz) kombu water (page 34)

2 tablespoons chopped coriander (cilantro) leaves

Preheat the oven to 220°C (425°F). Place the garlic cloves on a piece of foil and wrap like a little parcel. Place the garlic in the oven and roast for 20 minutes, or until the garlic is soft. Remove from the oven and set aside.

Place the cauliflower florets in a pot with just enough water to cover, then add 1 teaspoon of salt. Bring the water to the boil, then reduce the heat until the water is rapidly simmering. Cook the cauliflower for 12–15 minutes, or until very tender. Drain the cooked cauliflower and keep warm in the pot with a lid on it.

Cook the lamb by heating a large frying pan over medium–high heat with 1 teaspoon of tamari. Quickly add the onions and raw garlic and stir-fry for 2–3 minutes. Add the lamb and, using a wooden spoon, break up the lamb into small pieces. Season well with salt and pepper. Allow the lamb to cook for 5 minutes, stirring frequently, then add the cumin, coriander, curry powder and turmeric. Stir in well.

Stir the remaining 3 tablespoons of tamari into the water and add the liquid to the lamb. Cook the liquid down for about 10 minutes, or until it has formed a thick gravy. Taste for flavour, adding more salt and pepper to taste. Remove the pan from the heat and keep warm.

Finish off the cauliflower mash by placing the cooked florets into a small blender along with the flesh squeezed from the roasted garlic cloves. Season with salt and pepper and add the rosemary leaves along with the nutmeg and cumin. Blend until very smooth.

Place the warm lamb mixture in the base of a small pie dish and top with the cauliflower mash. Serve garnished with coriander.

Chicken and mint handheld salad

Sometimes it's the simple things that make the most impact and this salad does exactly that. When speed is important, nothing could be faster than a salad made of shredded roast chicken in a crunchy lettuce cup.

90 g (3¼ oz) shredded roast chicken breast, skin removed

200 g (7 oz) iceberg lettuce, broken into 2 natural cups

1 small handful mint leaves

2 teaspoons chopped chives

pinch of Himalayan salt and pepper

2 teaspoons Bridget's zesty dressing (page 28)

Holding 1 lettuce cup in your hand, fill with half the shredded chicken, some mint leaves, chives and a little pinch of salt and pepper.

Drizzle over 1 teaspoon of the zesty dressing. Repeat with the remaining ingredients and serve.

It's that easy!

TIP This is a great way to use up leftover roasted chicken.

Stir-fried chicken and basil salad on just-wilted spinach

This is a warm salad, need I say more? Dry-fried chicken breast sprinkled with an aromatic blend of warm spices, sitting on top of a bed of just-wilted spinach and topped with top notes of sweet basil. It is a flavour and textural sensation thanks to a finish of cracked rice cake.

100 g (3½ oz) chicken breast, sliced into strips

2 teaspoons Moroccan spice blend (page 42)

½ teaspoon Himalayan salt

½ teaspoon freshly ground black pepper

150 g (5½ oz) baby spinach

2 tablespoons low-sodium tamari

2 tablespoons water

1 teaspoon lemon juice

1 handful basil leaves

1 rice cake, broken into pieces

Heat a small non-stick frying pan over medium heat and, when hot, add the sliced chicken breast. Allow to cook, stir-frying for 1 minute. Sprinkle over the Moroccan spice blend and season with the salt and pepper. Continue to cook and stir for a further 3–4 minutes, or until the chicken is cooked through.

Remove the chicken from the pan and set aside. Add the spinach to the pan along with the tamari, water and lemon juice. Season with salt and pepper and cook for 30 seconds, turning the spinach over until it is just wilted.

Remove the spinach from the pan and place on a plate. Toss the cooked chicken with the basil leaves and crumbled rice cake and build on top of the spinach.

Season with salt and pepper and pour the liquid from the pan over top of the salad.

TIP Have you ever tried to eat 150 g (5½ oz) of raw spinach? It's daunting to say the least and despite it being very good for you and super low in calories, it's a terrifying prospect. Just wilting it in a hot pan for 30 seconds breaks the spinach down, making it more manageable, but as it breaks down it releases water, which helps to create a sauce for your salad. It also tastes great with simple seasoning.

Chicken dumpling soup with bok choy

Wholesome and warming, this broth is a wonderful elixir. The dumplings are tender and packed full of flavour and the broth is so simple to prepare – lunch will be done in no time.

400 ml (14 fl oz) kombu water (page 34)

½ teaspoon crushed ginger

2 tablespoons tamari

Himalayan salt and freshly ground black pepper

100 g (3½ oz) chicken dumplings, raw or cooked (page 61)

250 g (9 oz) small bok choy (pak choy), washed under cold running water

1 tablespoon finely chopped chives

1 tablespoon finely chopped coriander (cilantro) leaves

Heat the kombu water and ginger in a pot over medium–high heat until it comes gently to a simmer. Add the tamari and taste for flavour. The broth should be light and refreshing. Add salt and pepper to taste.

Drop the chicken dumplings into the pot and allow them to cook through for 5 minutes from raw or if already steamed, heat for a couple of minutes.

When just about ready to serve, add the bok choy and allow to cook for 1 minute so that the vegetables are just cooked through and still a bright green colour.

Serve the dish by adding the bok choy to a bowl along with the dumplings and pour the soup over the top. Sprinkle with the chives and coriander and serve.

TIP The chicken dumplings are taken straight from my healthy breakfast yum cha recipe (page 61) and can be gently boiled in this soup from raw, or added last minute to heat through if you have already steamed a whole heap for your breakfast!

TIP Bok choy – these wonderful Asian greens only need a few seconds in the hot broth to warm and cook through. Choose small bright green bok choy and discard the hard-outer leaves before adding to the soup.

Turkey, fennel and silverbeet broth

A restorative big bowl of slow-braised meat and vegetables is a wonderful thing, especially when the weather turns colder, and the sweaters and crockpots start to come out of the cupboards. This broth is so wonderfully flavoured, delicate yet robust, enchanting and comforting. Fennel has a big, bold aniseed flavour that for some can be overpowering. In this dish the fennel is slowly cooked, rendering that aniseed flavour much more palate pleasing.

200 g (7 oz) turkey meat, diced into bite-sized chunks

200 g (7 oz) fennel bulb, diced into bite-sized chunks

3 slices ginger

3 garlic cloves, sliced

1 tablespoon cumin seeds

600 ml (21 fl oz) kombu water (page 34)

Himalayan salt and freshly ground black pepper

340 g (11¾ oz) silverbeet (Swiss chard) leaves, thinly sliced

1 tablespoon finely chopped mint

1 small handful mint and coriander (cilantro) leaves

Add all the ingredients except for the silverbeet to a crockpot or slow cooker and cook on high for 4–5 hours, or until the turkey is tender. You can also cook this broth overnight over low heat for 8 hours.

When the cooking time is done, check the broth for flavour and season with salt and pepper to taste. Keep the broth warm while you prepare the silverbeet.

Bring a pot of water to the boil and add the sliced silverbeet. Cook for about 5 minutes or until the silverbeet is tender. Drain the water from the vegetables and add to two big bowls, then evenly divide the soup between each bowl.

Serve topped with mint and coriander. If you can purchase turkey breast, do so but you can also buy a turkey drumstick and carefully de-bone and dice the flesh. This needs a bit of time because the drumstick has lots of sinew that needs to be removed.

TIP You will ideally have a slow cooker or crockpot to make this recipe.

Chicken and Chinese cabbage in a tamari broth

Nothing satisfies the soul like a big steaming bowl of tasty soup. This soup is no exception and considering that it has no fat, sugar, carbs or gluten – it is a winner! Simple to make once you have taken the time to make a kombu broth, it's great for work or on the go as the raw cabbage can be kept separate until you are ready to heat up the broth.

600 ml (21 fl oz) kombu water (page 34)

2 tablespoons low-sodium tamari

1 teaspoon Himalayan salt

2 garlic cloves, crushed

200 g (7 oz) cooked chicken breast, shredded

200 g (7 oz) Chinese cabbage (wong bok), very finely shredded

3 tablespoons chopped coriander (cilantro)

3 tablespoons flat-leaf (Italian) parsley leaves

1 tablespoon chopped coriander (cilantro) root

1 small handful coriander (cilantro) and basil leaves

2 teaspoons ground wakame (page 40)

freshly ground black pepper

Heat the kombu water in a pot over medium–high heat. Add the tamari, salt and garlic and taste for flavour. The broth should taste light and fresh.

When the broth is bubbling gently, add the cabbage and heat for 1 minute. Remove the cabbage from the pot and place into two deep bowls. Add the chopped coriander root and chopped herbs and stir through followed by the shredded chicken.

Pour the hot broth over and top with the fresh herb leaves. Sprinkle over the ground wakame, and season with a little freshly ground black pepper.

Chicken and cauliflower sushi with a tamari dipping sauce

I had to close my eyes as I could have sworn when I bit into this nori wrapped delight that I was eating sushi. The cauliflower substitute for white rice is not only healthy for our bodies BUT it tastes amazing, and is so simple to make.

200 g (7 oz) raw cauliflower florets

pinch of Himalayan salt and freshly ground black pepper

1 sheet of pure nori (seaweed)

90 g (3¼ oz) cooked shredded chicken

1 tablespoon tamari and lime dipping sauce (page 31)

For the "sushi rice" cut the cauliflower florets into small pieces and add them to a food processor. Depending on the size of your food processor, you may have to work in batches as you don't want to overcrowd the bowl. Blend the cauliflower for 20–30 seconds, or until it resembles rice.

Microwave the cauliflower on high for 3 minutes, then season well with salt and pepper and stir through. Allow the cauliflower to cool for 20–30 minutes before filling the nori sheet.

To fill the nori sheet, place one sheet, shiny side down, on the bench and using the cooled cauliflower rice, spread it evenly across the sheet, leaving 2 cm (¾ in) at the top of the sheet empty for sealing the sushi.

Working at the end closest to you, add your chicken in a thin line from left to right, making sure to space and distribute the chicken evenly. This will help to roll your sushi.

Using a little water to wet your fingers, gently rub the top end of the nori sheet that does not have cauliflower. This will work to bind and seal your sushi when you roll.

Working again from the end closest to you, begin to roll your sushi up, encasing the filling as you go. Roll slowly and tightly so your sushi roll is strong and intact and when you get to the end, make sure to seal the wet end well.

continued overleaf

117

Chicken and cauliflower sushi with a tamari dipping sauce

If you have time, allow your sushi to rest in the refrigerator for 20–30 minutes as this will help with the cutting. When ready to eat, slice your sushi into 5–6 even pieces using a sharp knife.

For the tamari dipping sauce, mix together the ingredients for the dipping sauce in a bowl and taste for flavour, adding more lime juice and chilli to taste. Serve alongside the sliced sushi.

TIP In this recipe I give you ingredients for a simple chicken sushi, but you can swap and change the fillings to suit you. Add avocado or cucumber, or use fresh herbs, cooked flaked salmon, cooked crab or tinned tuna.

TIP When choosing your nori for your sushi, make sure to check the ingredients list as some nori sheets have added gluten, sugar, salt and preservatives. You just want pure seaweed or wakame for your nori sheets, so read up and shop around. I purchase my pure nori sheets in the health food aisle of the supermarket, but you can also check your Asian supermarket and your health food store.

Chicken fettuzzine

When you coin a phrase there is a certain level of excitement that goes along with creating something new. That's exactly how I felt about this chicken (fettuccine) fettuzzine dish after being challenged by someone who was sick of soggy zucchini noodles. This dish is delightful, super quick and simple and eliminates the watery noodle forever!

1 tablespoon low-sodium tamari, plus 1 teaspoon extra

100 g (3½ oz) lean minced (ground) chicken

1 teaspoon finely chopped garlic

1 teaspoon finely chopped ginger

Himalayan salt and freshly ground black pepper, to taste

1 teaspoon ground cumin

½ teaspoon ground coriander

2 teaspoons chopped coriander (cilantro) stalks

100 ml (3½ fl oz) kombu water (page 34)

250 g (9 oz) zucchini (courgette), cut or peeled into ribbons

1 small handful basil, mint or coriander (cilantro) leaves, finely shredded

Heat a large frying pan or wok over medium–high heat with a teaspoon of tamari. Quickly add the raw garlic and ginger and stir-fry for 30 seconds, then add the chicken. Using a wooden spoon, break up the chicken into small pieces. Season well with salt and pepper.

Allow the chicken to cook for 5 minutes, stirring frequently, then add the cumin and coriander powders along with the chopped coriander stalks. Stir in well.

Stir the remaining 1 tablespoon of tamari into the 100 ml (3½ fl oz) kombu water and add the liquid to the chicken. Cook the liquid down for about 5 minutes, or until it has formed a thick gravy. Taste for flavour, adding more salt and pepper to taste.

Toss in the zucchini ribbons and stir-fry briefly for 1 minute. Remove immediately from the heat. Add the finely shredded herbs and mix gently before serving in a deep bowl.

TIP I create my zucchini (courgette) ribbons with a rex potato peeler, which is a wide potato peeler and perfect for ribbons and speed peeling.

TIP Use lean minced (ground) chicken, beef or lamb for this dish.

The ultimate simple stir-fry

There is something about a hot wok and the simple addition of a few ingredients that makes not only a quick lunch or dinner but a wonderfully satisfying one. You can use minced (ground) beef or chicken in this stir-fry and it doesn't require a lot of your time, especially if you already have a jar of my sticky sauce in the fridge ready to go!

100 g (3½ oz) minced (ground) chicken or beef

½ teaspoon low-sodium tamari

1 teaspoon finely chopped garlic

1 teaspoon cumin powder

1 teaspoon ground coriander

2 tablespoons Bridget's sticky sauce (page 25)

4 tablespoons water

200 g (7 oz) Chinese or white cabbage, finely shredded

Himalayan salt and freshly ground black pepper

3 tablespoons chopped coriander (cilantro) or flat-leaf (Italian) parsley, including stalks

Make the meatballs by mixing together the turkey, garlic, ginger, rosemary, thyme, coriander stalks and 1 teaspoon of tamari. Add the salt and pepper and stir through.

Roll the meatballs into 6 equal-sized balls approximately 33 g (1 oz) in weight.

Heat a large frying pan over medium heat with 1 tablespoon of tamari and add the meatballs. Cook the balls for 5 minutes, rolling them often to ensure they cook evenly.

Add another tablespoon of tamari and toss in the fennel pieces. Continue to sauté and fry for a further 3 minutes, or until the fennel bulb softens a little and goes light brown.

Add the kombu water and bring to a simmer. Remove the meatballs from the pan. Add the choy sum and cook for 60 seconds, then remove from the heat. Taste the liquid for flavour, adding a bit of salt and pepper if needed.

Plate this dish by placing the vegetables and meatballs in a deep plate with a good splash of the liquid. Sprinkle over some of the coriander leaves and serve.

TIP You can swap the minced (ground) turkey with minced (ground) chicken and if you are struggling to find choy sum, you could also use bok choy (pak choy).

Chicken (zucchini) noodle soup

Wonderfully restorative is how I like to think of a steaming bowl of chicken soup, something that warms not just the insides but the soul as well. This version is a healthy broth made from kombu and wakame and finished with a good slap of zucchini noodles that are perfect for slurping.

600 ml (21 fl oz) kombu water (page 34)

2 tablespoons low-sodium tamari

1 teaspoon Himalayan salt

2 teaspoons finely chopped garlic

2 teaspoons finely chopped ginger

180 g (6½ oz) cooked chicken breast, shredded

1 large pinch of wakame pieces

3 tablespoons freshly chopped coriander (cilantro) or flat-leaf (Italian) parsley leaves

1 tablespoon freshly chopped coriander (cilantro) root

500 g (1 lb 2 oz) zucchini (courgette), peeled or sliced into noodles (page 263)

1 small handful coriander (cilantro) and basil leaves

freshly ground black pepper

Heat the kombu water in a pot over medium–high heat. Add the tamari, salt, garlic and ginger, and taste for flavour. The broth should taste light and fresh.

Heat the soup until it almost comes to the boil, then add the shredded chicken meat, wakame and chopped coriander and parsley leaves.

Into 2 large deep bowls, evenly distribute the zucchini noodles and pour over the hot soup and chicken. Top the soup with a few extra fresh herbs and a good grinding of black pepper.

Serve while still steaming.

TIP This recipe is good for using up cooked chicken.

Turkey meatballs with choy sum and fennel stew

These meatballs are so full of flavour. The herbs complement the turkey and work beautifully with the lightly braised vegetables, making for a delicious lunch.

200 g (7 oz) lean minced (ground) turkey

2 teaspoons finely chopped garlic

1 tablespoon grated ginger

2 teaspoons fresh or dried rosemary

1 teaspoon fresh or dried thyme leaves

1 teaspoon chopped coriander (cilantro) stalks

3 tablespoons low-sodium tamari, plus 1 teaspoon extra

1 teaspoon Himalayan salt

1 teaspoon freshly ground black pepper

200 g (7 oz) fennel bulb, chopped into bite-sized pieces

300 ml (10½ fl oz) kombu water (page 34)

320 g (11¼ oz) choy sum, washed, and chopped into pieces

1 tablespoon chopped coriander (cilantro) leaves, to serve

Make the meatballs by mixing together the turkey, garlic, ginger, rosemary, thyme, coriander stalks and 1 teaspoon of tamari. Add the salt and pepper and stir through.

Roll the meatballs into 6 equal-sized balls approximately 33 g (1 oz) in weight.

Heat a large frying pan over medium heat with 1 tablespoon of tamari and add the meatballs. Cook the balls for 5 minutes, rolling them often to ensure they cook evenly.

Add another tablespoon of tamari and toss in the fennel pieces. Continue to sauté and fry for a further 3 minutes, or until the fennel bulb softens a little and goes light brown.

Add the kombu water and bring to a simmer. Remove the meatballs from the pan. Add the choy sum and cook for 60 seconds, then remove from the heat. Taste the liquid for flavour, adding a bit of salt and pepper if needed.

Plate this dish by placing the vegetables and meatballs in a deep plate with a good splash of the liquid. Sprinkle over some of the coriander leaves and serve.

TIP You can swap the minced (ground) turkey with minced (ground) chicken and if you are struggling to find choy sum, you could also use bok choy (pak choy).

Turkey stir-fry with a fennel and orange salad

A tender stir-fry feels like such a treat when combined with this fabulous and simple-to-put-together fennel and orange salad.

160 g (5¾ oz) silverbeet (Swiss chard), washed and sliced into thin strips

Himalayan salt and freshly ground black pepper

2 teaspoons low-sodium tamari

100 g (3½ oz) raw turkey breast meat, sliced into thin strips

2 teaspoons finely chopped ginger

1 teaspoon finely chopped garlic

100 g (3½ oz) fennel bulb, finely sliced on a mandolin (page 19)

½ orange, peeled and segmented

½ tablespoon Bridget's zesty dressing (page 28)

1 tablespoon shredded baby basil leaves

1 tablespoon shredded coriander (cilantro) leaves

Bring a pot of water to the boil with a couple of pinches of salt. Add the silverbeet and cook for 3–4 minutes, or until tender.

Heat a large non-stick wok or frying pan over medium–high heat and add the tamari followed by the turkey, ginger and garlic. Season with salt and pepper and stir-fry for a couple of minutes, or until the turkey is tender.

Drain the water from the silverbeet and add the silverbeet to the pan. Stir-fry together with the turkey for 1 minute.

Combine the salad ingredients by tossing the fennel and orange with the zesty dressing and mix through the basil and coriander leaves thoroughly.

Season with a little salt and pepper and serve alongside the silverbeet and turkey.

Spiced chicken and wilted spinach

A warm, slightly wilted salad is a fabulous and quick lunch idea that is low in calories and high in flavour.

1 tablespoon Bridget's sticky sauce (page 25)

1 garlic clove, crushed

1 teaspoon crushed ginger

1 green chilli, finely chopped (optional)

100 g (3½ oz) lean minced (ground) chicken

Himalayan salt and freshly ground black pepper, to taste

1 teaspoon ground cumin

1 teaspoon ground allspice

2 teaspoons chopped coriander (cilantro) stalks

100 ml (3½ fl oz) water

150 g (5½ oz) baby spinach leaves

1 small handful mint and basil leaves

Heat a large frying pan or wok over medium—high heat with the sticky sauce. Quickly add the raw garlic, ginger and chilli, if using, and stir-fry for 30 seconds. Add the chicken and using a wooden spoon, break up the chicken into small pieces. Season well with salt and pepper.

Allow the chicken to cook for 5 minutes, stirring frequently, then add the cumin and allspice powders along with the chopped coriander stalks. Stir in well.

Add the water to the chicken and cook the liquid down for about 5 minutes, or until it has formed a thick gravy. Taste for flavour, adding more salt and pepper to taste.

Toss in three-quarters of the spinach leaves and stir to combine very briefly, then remove the pan from the heat.

Plate up the chicken and spinach along with the liquid from the pan.

Top with spinach leaves, mint and basil and a grinding of salt and freshly ground pepper.

Sticky chicken and zucchini chips

As the name might suggest, sticky chicken is 'finger licking good'! Combined with zucchini chips, this is a quick and easy dish that tastes incredible.

100 g (3½ oz) chicken breast, thinly sliced

1 tablespoon Bridget's sticky sauce (page 25)

350 g (12 oz) zucchini (courgette), sliced into chips

Himalayan salt and freshly ground black pepper

1 tablespoon oil-free pesto (page 26)

1 lemon wedge, to serve

.

In a bowl, add the chicken breast and spoon over the sticky sauce. Mix the chicken to ensure it is well covered in the sauce. You could do this step the night before to marinate the chicken because it helps the flavour develop.

Season the zucchini chips with salt and pepper. If using an air fryer, preheat the air fryer to 200°C (400°F) or preheat the oven to 200°C (400°F).

For the air fryer, add a small piece of baking paper to the basket and lay the chicken breast in a single layer. Cook for 8–9 minutes, or until the chicken is cooked but still tender. If your air fryer has a two-level wire rack, lay the zucchini chips on top and cook at the same time as the chicken, or cook them separately for 8–10 minutes.

For the oven, lay a piece of baking paper on a roasting tray and add the chicken and zucchini chips in a single layer. Cook for 15 minutes, or until the chicken is cooked and the zucchini is tender.

Serve the chicken and chips with a sprinkle of salt and pepper and a side of the oil-free pesto.

TIP I used an air fryer to achieve my wonderfully moist results but you can also make this in an oven and I have included directions for both methods.

Chicken, basil and zucchini stir-fry

A quick and simple dish with wonderful flavours. Stir-fried lightly with an oil-free pesto and fresh basil leaves to finish. Clean and uncomplicated!

2 teaspoons low-sodium tamari

1 teaspoon finely chopped garlic

1 tablespoon finely chopped ginger

100 g (3½ oz) chicken breast, thinly sliced

Himalayan salt and freshly ground black pepper

350 g (12 oz) zucchini (courgette), sliced in half lengthways and thinly sliced into pieces

3 tablespoons oil-free pesto (page 26)

1 small handful baby basil leaves

Heat a large frying pan or wok over medium–high heat. Add the tamari, garlic and ginger and stir-fry for 1 minute.

Add the chicken and stir-fry for 2 minutes, then add the zucchini. Stir the zucchini, season with salt and pepper and fry for a couple of minutes, stirring continuously.

Add the pesto and stir through, then remove the pan from the heat.

Add the basil leaves and a little more seasoning and serve.

Chicken nuggets on slaw

Healthy chicken nuggets? Yes, you can! Use a rice cake, blitzed and crumbed to give the chicken a bit of crumb and a fabulous fresh and zingy slaw to accompany the nuggets.

1 rice cake, blended to crumbs

Himalayan salt and freshly ground black pepper

¼ teaspoon allspice

¼ teaspoon paprika

¼ teaspoon cumin powder

¼ teaspoon pure garlic powder

100 g (3½ oz) chicken breast, cut into cubes

1 small handful coriander (cilantro) leaves

1 small handful mint leaves

1 small handful basil leaves

200 g (7 oz) finely shredded cabbage

1 small green apple, finely shredded

2 tablespoons Bridget's zesty dressing (page 28)

1 lemon wedge

In a shallow bowl, mix together the rice cake crumbs, a pinch each of salt and pepper, and the allspice, paprika, cumin powder and garlic powder.

Wet the chicken breast cubes with water, then lay them through the spiced rice cake mixture, pressing as much crumb on to the chicken pieces as possible.

If using an air fryer, preheat to 200°C (400°F) for 2 minutes. Lay the crumbed chicken in the fryer basket and cook for 8–9 minutes, or until the chicken is cooked through.

If cooking in the oven, preheat the oven to 200°C (400°F). Lay the chicken on a small baking paper lined tray and bake for 12–15 minutes, or until cooked through.

While the chicken cooks, make the slaw by finely chopping half of the coriander, basil and mint leaves while leaving the rest as whole leaves.

In a bowl, mix together the herbs, cabbage and apple, and stir through the zesty dressing. Taste for flavour and season with salt and pepper.

Serve the slaw alongside the chicken nuggets with a wedge of lemon.

Pulled chicken fast or slow cooked

As this dish cooks and the spices begin to bloom, the smell emanating from your slow or pressure cooker will be incredible and you will know exactly why this is delicious!

120 ml (4 fl oz) kombu water (page 34)

120 ml (4 fl oz) low-sodium tamari

150 ml (5 fl oz) strong black coffee

1 tablespoon freshly ground black pepper

2 teaspoons allspice

2 teaspoons cinnamon

2 teaspoons fresh or dried basil or thyme

1 teaspoon chilli flakes

1 teaspoon paprika

8 garlic cloves, finely chopped

3 tablespoons freshly grated ginger

2 onions, peeled and diced

1.5 kg (3 lb 5 oz) chicken breasts, skin removed

Whisk together the kombu water with the tamari, coffee, black pepper, garlic and ginger. Whisk in the allspice, cinnamon, basil or thyme, chilli flakes and paprika. Stir in the garlic and ginger.

Place the onions and chicken breast into the bowl of your pressure cooker or slow cooker and pour over the liquid mixture. Stir to combine.

If using a pressure cooker, cook over medium–high for 30 minutes, once the steam has built up, or as per manufacturer's instructions for cooking a pot roast.

If using a slow cooker, cook the chicken on low for 6–8 hours, or until tender, or as per manufacturer's instructions for cooking a pot roast. If using a heavy-based pot, cook over low heat for 3–4 hours, stirring occasionally to make sure the meat doesn't stick to the pot.

When the meat is tender, check the sauce for flavour, adding more tamari or pepper if necessary. If the sauce seems a little watery, you can bring the chicken liquid to the boil and allow it reduce in volume until the sauce thickens to your liking.

Pull the chicken when cool enough to handle, and serve with your preferred accompaniments and some of the reduced chicken sauce poured over the chicken.

TIP This dish can be prepared and stored in portions and frozen for up to 1 month.

Chicken and fennel tagine

Fragrant and aromatic, this dish is wonderfully satisfying. The lemons add a delicious flavour that complements the fennel and silverbeet really well.

1 pinch of saffron threads (about 20 strands)

2 garlic cloves, crushed

1 teaspoon Himalayan salt

1 teaspoon ground cumin

½ teaspoon paprika

½ teaspoon turmeric

100 g (3½ oz) chicken or turkey breast, sliced into bite-sized cubes

½ teaspoon low-sodium tamari

100 g (3½ oz) fennel bulb, cut into small dice

¼ preserved lemon (page 253), finely diced

200 ml (7 fl oz) kombu water (page 34)

freshly ground black pepper

160 g (5¾ oz) silverbeet (Swiss chard) or rainbow chard, well washed and sliced into strips

2 tablespoons chopped coriander (cilantro) leaves

Soak the saffron strands in 2 tablespoons of boiling water for 10 minutes. In a small bowl mix together the saffron and soaking water, garlic, salt, cumin, paprika and turmeric. Rub this mixture all over the chicken or turkey and allow it to marinate for at least 4 hours. You can also leave the meat to marinate overnight to allow the flavours time to develop.

Heat a small heavy-based pot, pan or tagine over medium heat. Add the tamari and fennel bulb and gently sauté for a couple of minutes. Add the marinated meat along with all the spices and liquid and continue to cook for another minute.

Add the preserved lemons and the kombu water, bring to a simmer and let the chicken and fennel cook for 15 minutes. Add the silverbeet and cook for a further 5 minutes, or until the chard is tender. Taste for flavour and season with salt and pepper to taste.

Serve the tagine sprinkled with coriander.

TIP You can use chicken or turkey breast for this recipe.

Stir-fried scallops and broccolini

Scallops and broccolini are a perfect match. Both are a little sweet and delicate. This simple stir-fry takes only minutes to make and is a deliciously satisfying meal.

1 tablespoon tamari and lime dipping sauce (page 31)

1 garlic clove, finely chopped

1 teaspoon finely grated ginger

100 g (3½ oz) scallops, fresh or defrosted

Himalayan salt and freshly ground black pepper

200 g (7 oz) broccolini, long stalks removed and discarded

1 small handful coriander (cilantro), mint or basil leaves

2 teaspoons ground wakame (page 40)

Heat a pot of water over medium–high heat until it begins to boil gently.

In the meantime, heat a large frying pan or wok over medium heat and add 1 tablespoon of the tamari sauce, along with the garlic and ginger. Allow these to gently fry for a couple of minutes, stirring frequently.

Add the scallops and season with salt and pepper. Cook the scallops briefly for 1 minute, stirring constantly and then remove the pan from the heat.

Add the broccolini to the pot of water and cook for 1 minute, then remove the broccolini from the pot with a slotted spoon (reserving the water). Add the broccolini straight into the scallop pan and place the pan back over medium–high heat.

Stirring constantly, add another tablespoon of the tamari sauce and fry the contents of the pan for 1 minute. Add a couple of tablespoons of the water you cooked the broccolini in and season with a little salt and pepper. Serve immediately, tossed with the fresh herbs and sprinkled with the wakame

TIP Broccolini is the cousin to the larger, more common broccoli. Its sweet mild flavour lends itself well to this dish. If you can find broccolini give it a try. You can use broccoli, just cut it into small florets.

TIP Choose fresh scallops if you can find them or thaw frozen scallops for a couple of minutes under cold running water. Pat them dry before cooking.

Salmon ceviche

Fresh fish covered in citrus and served thinly sliced is an exceptionally easy and wonderfully delicious dish. This style of raw fish is most common in Mexico and South America, where they use lime to marinate and chilli to add a sliver of heat.

100–150 g fresh salmon fillet, skin and bones removed

1 tablespoon fresh lime juice

½ tablespoon fresh lemon juice

½ teaspoon fresh chilli, finely chopped

1 teaspoon finely chopped coriander, mint or basil

1 teaspoon ground wakame (page 40)

Himalayan salt and freshly ground black pepper

2 tablespoons tamari and lime and dipping sauce, to serve (page 31)

Cover the salmon fillet in cling film or place in a plastic bag and pop in the freezer for 30 minutes. This will greatly assist you in slicing it as thin as possible.

Using a sharp knife, slice the salmon as thinly as possible and lay the slices onto a plate.

Drizzle the lime and lemon over the salmon and allow to marinate for 20 minutes.

Sprinkle over the chilli, fresh herbs and wakame, and season with a little salt and pepper. Serve alongside a fresh lettuce salad and the lime and tamari dipping sauce.

TIP You will need to start this recipe 1 hour before you intend to eat and ideally consume within a couple of hours of making.

Shellfish and watercress

This is delicious because it is light and tender with the subtle flavour of the ocean. It has an amazing flavour and is fun to eat! If you can't find watercress you can use baby spinach or baby bok choy (pak choy) instead.

170 g (6 oz) watercress, large stalks removed (weigh after removing stalks)

150 g (5½ oz) cockle, clam or pipi meat (about 30 cockles)

1 garlic clove, peeled and finely chopped

Himalayan salt and freshly ground black pepper

1 tablespoon finely chopped coriander (cilantro) stalks

1 small handful coriander (cilantro) leaves, finely chopped

Wash the watercress well by rubbing the leaves together and breaking up the sprigs so they are easier to eat. Rinse in plenty of cold running water, discarding any brown or aged leaves.

Heat a large non-stick wok or frying pan over medium–high heat and add the cockles. Place a lid over the cockles and allow them to start to steam themselves open. Turn the heat down to medium and allow the cockles to continue to steam open, removing each cockle as soon as the shell springs open and setting the cockle aside in a bowl.

There should be about 125 ml (4 fl oz/½ cup) of natural liquid in the base of the pan, if not, add enough water so it comes up to about 125 ml (4 fl oz/½ cup). Add the garlic and watercress to the liquid and cook for about 2 minutes, or until the watercress is still vibrant green but tender to the bite. Season the watercress with salt and pepper and sprinkle in the chopped coriander stalks.

Place the watercress in a deep bowl, add the cockles on top of the watercress, then pour the liquid from the pan over the top of the cockles until it creates a little pool of liquid in the plate. Sprinkle over the coriander leaves and season with a little salt and pepper before serving.

TIP I used New Zealand little neck clams or cockles as they are called but you can also use pipis or vongole. The best way to measure how many clams you will need to reach your portion size is to weigh one, flesh only, and then give an accurate estimate of how many you will need to make up 100 g (3½ oz) of meat. I calculated 4–5 g (⅛ oz) per clam, so I used 30 clams.

Mussel broth with zucchini noodles

A simple mussel broth that makes the most out of their wonderful flavour. Combined with zucchini noodles, this is a great filling dish for lunch.

300 ml (10½ fl oz) kombu water (page 34)

2 tablespoons low-sodium tamari

1 pinch of saffron, about 20 strands

2 roasted garlic cloves, mashed

1 tablespoon freshly grated ginger

1 teaspoon turmeric

2 cm (¾ in) piece of lemongrass, smashed with the flat of a knife

Himalayan salt and freshly ground black pepper

100 g (3½ oz) raw mussel meat, chopped into small pieces

2 teaspoons finely chopped coriander (cilantro) stalks

350 g (12 oz) zucchini (courgette), peeled into noodles

1 small handful mint and coriander (cilantro) leaves

Heat the kombu water, tamari, saffron, garlic, ginger, turmeric and lemongrass in a pot over medium heat. Allow it to come to a gentle simmer and taste for flavour, adding a little salt and pepper.

Add the mussel meat and coriander stalks and cook for 1 minute, then remove from the heat.

Season the zucchini noodles with salt and pepper and add to a deep bowl. Pour the hot mussel broth over the top and serve topped with mint and coriander leaves.

Chilli and lime prawn skewers

A wonderful lunchtime dish of sticky delicious prawns (shrimp) and a fresh flavoursome salad. The crunch of the salad is a lovely texture that complements the sweet nature of just-cooked prawns.

1 long red chilli, seeds discarded, skin finely chopped

1 lime, juiced

1 teaspoon finely chopped garlic

1 teaspoon freshly grated ginger

1 tablespoon Bridget's sticky sauce (page 25)

100 g (3½ oz) raw prawn (shrimp) tails

Himalayan salt and freshly ground black pepper

100 g (3½ oz) fennel bulb, finely sliced

½ large green apple, finely chopped into matchsticks

¼ finely chopped preserved lemon

2 tablespoons Bridget's zesty dressing (page 28)

1 small handful mint and coriander (cilantro) leaves

100 g (3½ oz) rocket (arugula) lettuce

1 teaspoon low-sodium tamari

Stir together the chilli, lime juice, garlic, ginger and sticky sauce and use this mixture to cover the prawn tails.

Thread the prawn tails onto a couple of bamboo skewers and season with salt and pepper. At this point you can choose to marinate the prawns in the sauce for 30–60 minutes to give the flavours time to develop, or you could freeze the prawns to defrost when ready to cook.

Make the fennel salad by mixing together the fennel, apple and preserved lemon and drizzle over about half of the zesty dressing. Toss through the fresh herbs and the rocket lettuce.

Heat a large non-stick frying pan over medium–high heat and add 1 teaspoon tamari. Add the prawn skewers and cook quickly for 30–40 seconds before turning the skewers and cooking for a further 30–40 seconds until just cooked. Serve alongside the salad with the extra zesty dressing for drizzling.

I suggest you select raw prawn tails over cooked. The flavour is superior to pre-cooked prawns and they only take a few seconds to cook! You can buy frozen ones and defrost by letting them sit in a bowl of cold water for 10–15 minutes before cooking, or rinse them under cold running water.

TIP A little reminder that chilli can inflame the gut in some people, so go carefully if you are new to chillies.

A FAMILY AFFAIR MADE FRESH WHENEVER POSSIBLE.

Dinner is often a rushed affair in our house, with people coming and going at all different times of the day and night. Despite the busy nature of our home, we try to sit down together as often as we can. There is nothing quite as satisfying as sharing a meal, whether it's at the dining table or perched on stools at the kitchen counter.

In this chapter, I showcase my fondness for seafood and share more of my poultry recipes. As with the other chapters, feel free to swap chicken for turkey, and swap vegetables out if you find that something is not in season or budget friendly. Herbs are also interchangeable but I suggest you use fresh herbs whenever possible as the flavour is superior to that of dried herbs.

Dinner

Grilled fish and mash with sticky sauce and pesto

This recipe may seem daunting at first, but it's made up of components that are worth you making and having on hand at all times to help you with your healthy living journey!

Cauliflower mash

140 g (5 oz) raw cauliflower florets

1 teaspoon finely chopped rosemary leaves

pinch of nutmeg

pinch of cumin

125 g (4½ oz) piece of thick white fish fillet

1 lime wedge

1 teaspoon finely chopped coriander (cilantro) stalks

1 tablespoon Bridget's sticky sauce (page 25)

1 tablespoon oil-free pesto (page 26)

Preheat the oven grill (broiler) on high and line a small roasting tray with a piece of non-stick baking paper.

For the cauliflower mash, place the cauliflower florets in a pot with just enough water to cover and season with a pinch of salt. Bring the water to the boil, then turn down the heat until the water is rapidly simmering. Cook the cauliflower for 12–15 minutes or until very tender.

Drain the cooked cauliflower from the water, and keep warm in the pot with a lid on it. Lay the fish fillet into the roasting tray and squeeze the lime over the top. Season with salt and pepper and sprinkle over half of the chopped coriander stalks. Place in the oven and cook for 6–10 minutes, or until just cooked through and beginning to flake gently.

While the fish cooks, blend the cauliflower in a small food processor or with a hand blender until very smooth. Add the rosemary leaves, nutmeg and cumin and season to taste with a little salt and pepper.

Place the mash on the base of the plate and spoon a little of the pesto onto the mash. Top the mash with the cooked fish. Sprinkle with the remaining coriander stalks and drizzle some of the sticky sauce around the plate.

TIP Choose a thick slice of white fish as opposed to a thin fillet. The thicker fillet responds to grilling (broiling) better and will remain moist and tender as you eat it. Fish that I like to use are barramundi, snapper and cod.

Fish tagine

The spice profile of Morocco suits this quick fish dish perfectly. It's aromatic, flavoursome and totally satisfying. It only takes 15 minutes to prepare once the spice blend and saffron water are complete, which makes it a real winner when you are pressed for time but still want to eat something amazing!

1 teaspoon cumin seeds

140 g (5 oz) zucchini (courgette) or cauliflower, cut into chunks

200 ml (7 fl oz) saffron water (page 33)

¾ teaspoon turmeric powder

2 teaspoons Moroccan spice blend (page 42)

125 g (4½ oz) firm white fish, cut into chunks

1 teaspoon lemon zest

1 teaspoon ground wakame (page 40)

1 lemon wedge, to serve

1 teaspoon finely chopped coriander (cilantro) or fenugreek leaves

Heat a small frying pan over medium heat and add the cumin seeds. Allow the cumin seeds to brown gently for a couple of minutes, then add the zucchini or cauliflower.

Cook for 1 minute, stirring occasionally, then add 4 tablespoons of the saffron water and the turmeric powder. Allow the liquid to bubble a little, then add the fish followed by the Moroccan spice blend. Stir gently to distribute the spices, then add the rest of the saffron water.

Allow the mixture to cook for 5–10 minutes, or until the fish and vegetables are tender and the saffron water has reduced down to a lovely gravy.

Season with salt and pepper and sprinkle over the lemon zest and wakame. Serve with a wedge of lemon on the side.

TIP Make saffron water (page 31) in bulk and store in the refrigerator for use in curries and rich sauces.

Prawn and zucchini noodles in a kombu broth

At the risk of stating the obvious … it has prawns (shrimp)! Big, fat, juicy prawn tails, which are just cooked through to retain that wonderful moisture associated with well-prepared crustacea. It also incorporates the wildly popular zucchini noodles, or zoodles as they often called, where eating 300 g (10½ oz) of zucchini is remarkably easy and delicious. Combine this with an unashamedly tasty kombu broth and some fresh herbs and dinner is served!

½ tablespoon low-sodium tamari

2 garlic cloves, finely chopped

5 mm (¼ in) piece of ginger, grated

150 g (5½ oz) raw prawn (shrimp) tails, peeled

Himalayan salt and freshly ground black pepper

300 g (10½ oz) raw zucchini (courgette), peeled into noodles

200 ml (7 fl oz) kombu broth (page 34)

1 small handful basil leaves, finely chopped

1 tablespoon ground wakame (page 40)

½ lemon, cut into a wedge with the rest juiced

Place a non-stick wok or frying pan over medium heat and add the tamari, quickly followed by the garlic and ginger. Stir-fry constantly for 1 minute without letting the garlic and ginger burn.

Add the prawns, a pinch each of salt and pepper, a sprinkle of wakame and a squeeze of lemon juice. Stir-fry for 1 minute, or until the prawns are just cooked through and have gone from translucent to opaque in colour with a light orange hue. Take the prawns and any liquid from the pan and set aside.

Using the same pan, place it back over a medium–high heat and add the zucchini noodles. Season well with salt and pepper and sprinkle over the chopped basil and another sprinkle of ground wakame. Stir-fry VERY briefly, allowing the noodles to cook for 10 seconds before adding the kombu broth. Cook for a further 20 seconds, or until the kombu broth just starts to bubble.

Place the noodles in a bowl. Add the prawns, sprinkled with a little ground wakame and some of the chopped basil. Serve with a lemon wedge on the side.

TIP ALWAYS buy raw (or green) prawns. They are quick and easy to cook and your tastebuds will be forever grateful. Pre-cooked prawns' flavour is inferior and the prawn meat is so much drier than when you cook them yourself.

Fish 'n' chips

Who doesn't love fish and chips? Growing up, Thursday night was always fish and chips night in our house, where a grease-laden parcel of fish and chips graced our kitchen table. Although this was seen as treat, I was always left with a mouth full of oil and a body that was not prepared to do anything after that monstrous feed. This is a delicious and fresh take on my Thursday night staple. Using a grilled fish covered in rice cracker crumbs, it's accompanied by baked zucchini chips and a sweet basil and lemon pesto.

250 g (9 oz) zucchini (courgette), cut into chips

2 tablespoons oil-free pesto (page 26)

1 plain rice cake, blended into fine crumbs

125 g (4½ oz) piece white fish fillet, medium to firm

1 teaspoon ground wakame (page 40)

1 lemon wedge

Preheat the oven to 220°C (425°F) and line a baking tray with baking paper. Place the zucchini chips in a single layer on the baking tray, leaving a little space for the fish fillet. Sprinkle the chips with salt and pepper and drizzle over 1 tablespoon of oil-free pesto. Bake for 15–20 minutes, or until golden and crisp.

Pat a little water over the fish fillet and, using the rice cracker crumbs, pat them onto the fish fillet to form a crust. Season with salt and pepper and the ground wakame.

About 10 minutes into the baking of the zucchini chips, add the fish to the baking tray. Cook for a further 5–10 minutes, or until the chips are lightly golden and the fish is just cooked through and flakes away when touched with a fork.

Serve with a lemon wedge and side of pesto for dipping the chips.

TIP Use a firm white fish that doesn't fall apart when you cook it. The thicker the better. If you are using frozen fish, allow the fish to defrost overnight in the refrigerator for best defrosted fish results.

Sticky salmon on broccoli rice

Attach the word sticky to food and I instantly want to eat it. Nothing could be truer when it comes to this recipe and its absolute juicy sticky tenderness. Simple and delicious, this is mono eating at its tastiest.

100 g (3½ oz) fresh salmon, skin left on

1 tablespoon Bridget's sticky sauce (page 25)

1 portion of broccoli rice (page 266)

3 mint leaves, very thinly sliced

¼ sheet nori, folded and sliced very thinly

Himalayan salt

freshly ground black pepper

Cut the salmon into bite-sized pieces and place in a small bowl along with the sticky sauce. Cover the salmon well with the sauce. Leave the salmon to marinate for 30–60 minutes.

Preheat the air fryer to 160°C (315°F) or preheat the oven to 200°C (400°F).

If using the air fryer, place the salmon into the air fryer and cook for 6–7 minutes, or until golden and just cooked through.

If using the oven, place the salmon on a small baking tray lined with baking paper and cook for 10 minutes.

Serve the warm broccoli rice in a bowl topped with the salmon. Sprinkle over a little more salt and pepper and finish with the chopped mint and nori.

TIP I use an air fryer to cook the salmon but you can also cook the salmon in the oven.

Grilled fish on curried cabbage and apple

The ideal meal when you need a variety of flavours and textures in a hurry. Aromatic and crunchy while mild, soft and mellow, thanks to a delicately cooked piece of fish.

125 g (4½ oz) piece white fish fillet

2 teaspoons freshly grated ginger

½ lemon or lime, juiced plus wedges, to serve

Himalayan salt and freshly ground black pepper

1 teaspoon cumin seeds

1 teaspoon fennel seeds

1 teaspoon low-sodium tamari

1 garlic clove, crushed

1 teaspoon cumin powder

1 teaspoon ground coriander

1 teaspoon curry powder

pinch of chilli powder

150 g (5½ oz) white cabbage, finely shredded

4 tablespoons kombu water (page 34)

½ green apple, finely chopped into matchsticks

2 tablespoons mint leaves, finely shredded

Preheat the oven grill (broiler) to high and line a roasting tray with baking paper. Place the fish into the roasting tray. Add ½ teaspoon of grated ginger to the top of the fish and squeeze over a bit of the lemon or lime juice. Season with salt and pepper.

Place the fish under the grill and cook for 4–5 minutes, or until the fish flakes away when touched by a fork.

In the meantime, heat a wok or large frying pan over medium–high heat and dry toast the cumin and fennel seeds until they begin to pop. Add the tamari and the rest of the ginger and garlic and stir-fry briefly. Add the cumin, coriander and curry powders. Stir briefly, then add the cabbage and stir the spices through the cabbage.

Continue stir-frying for 1 minute, then add the water and season well with salt and pepper. Cook for a further 1 minute, then remove the pan from the heat and toss through the apple and chopped herbs.

Serve the cooked fish on top of the curried cabbage and apple, with a side of lime for squeezing.

TIP Choose a thick piece of white fish like snapper or barramundi which cooks up more tender and satisfying than a thin piece, because it retains more moisture.

Jamaican spiced fish curry with roasted cauliflower rice

The heady intoxicating spices so popular in Jamaica work well to flavour the fish while the nutty roasted cauliflower rice is next level wonderful. To help improve the flavour of the curry, marinate your fish in the lime juice and spices overnight in the refrigerator. You can replace the fish with prawns if you prefer.

300 g (10½ oz) firm white fish fillets, cut into bite-sized chunks

1 lime, juiced

2 teaspoons curry powder

½ teaspoon turmeric

½ teaspoon allspice

2 teaspoons low-sodium tamari, added to 150 ml (5 fl oz) water

4 tablespoons ground wakame (page 40)

2 lime wedges, to serve

Roasted cauliflower rice

280 g (10 oz) raw cauliflower florets, roughly chopped

Himalayan salt and freshly ground black pepper

1 lemon, zested and juiced

2 small garlic cloves, peeled and finely chopped

2 tablespoons finely chopped flat-leaf (Italian) parsley leaves

Preheat the oven to 200°C (400°F) and line a baking tray with baking paper.

Place the cauliflower florets into a food processor and pulse until the cauliflower resembles rice. (Don't blend it for too long or you will end up with a purée!)

Transfer the cauliflower rice onto the baking tray and smooth it out into single layer. Season with salt and pepper and place in the oven. Bake for 18–20 minutes, or until the rice is lightly coloured and tender to the bite.

While the cauliflower bakes, prepare the curry by adding the fish chunks to a small bowl and cover with the lime juice. Sprinkle over the curry powder, turmeric and allspice and season with salt and pepper. Stir to combine.

Heat a small non-stick pot over medium heat. Add the fish and cook for 30 seconds. Add the tamari mixed with water, and 2 tablespoons of wakame. Bring to a gentle simmer to allow the curry to cook gently until the liquid reduces and thickens slightly. Taste for flavour, adding more seasoning, wakame or lime juice to taste. Place a lid on the pot and remove from the heat.

Finish off the cauliflower rice by adding the lemon juice, lemon zest, garlic and parsley to small bowl and mixing well. Stir through the cauliflower.

Serve the cauliflower rice on a plate, topped with the curry. Add another sprinkle of wakame and a lime wedge for squeezing.

Fish dumpling and bok choy soup

This is such a wonderful way to get more lean, healthy white fish into your diet in such a delicious and simple way. In this recipe we make some fabulous fish balls, then poach them in the most wondrous broth. It's all finished off with tender Asian greens for a super satisfying lunch or dinner.

Fish dumplings

125 g (4½ oz) skinless, boneless white fish fillets, diced

½ teaspoon Himalayan salt

pinch of white pepper

1 teaspoon inulin powder

½ teaspoon ground wakame (page 40)

1 tablespoon kombu water (page 34)

Soup

350 ml (12 fl oz) kombu water

1 tablespoon freshly crushed ginger

2 garlic cloves, finely chopped

1 tablespoon low-sodium tamari

1 tablespoon wakame

200 g (7 oz) small bok choy (pak choy), washed under running water

1 tablespoon finely chopped chives

1 tablespoon finely chopped coriander (cilantro) leaves

Prepare the fish balls by placing the diced fish in a food processor and blending on low speed for 1–2 minutes, or until the fish turns into a paste. Add the salt, white pepper, inulin, ground wakame and water and blend to combine.

Using clean hands and a small bowl of water to dip your fingers into, roll the fish paste into 4–8 even-sized balls. Set aside in the fridge while you prepare the soup.

Heat the kombu water in a pot until it is just bubbling and add the ginger, garlic, tamari and wakame. Taste the soup for flavour, adding a little salt and pepper if needed.

Carefully lower the fish balls into the soup and cook the dumplings for 4–5 minutes, or until cooked through. Add the bok choy and cook for a further 1 minute.

Serve the dish by adding the bok choy to a bowl along with the dumplings and pour the soup over top. Sprinkle with the chives and coriander and serve!

Fish cooked in paper on kombu broccolini

Sealing a delicate food like salmon in paper before popping it into the oven helps to lock in all that wonderful moisture. Adding toppings like lemon and herbs helps to flavour and add excitement!

200 ml (7 fl oz) kombu water (page 34)

1 teaspoon grated ginger, plus ½ teaspoon extra

1 garlic clove, finely chopped

2 teaspoons ground wakame (page 40)

1 tablespoon low-sodium tamari

125 g (4½ oz) white fish fillet or 100 g (3½ oz) salmon fillet

Himalayan salt and freshly ground black pepper

½ lemon, plus 1 wedge

1 teaspoon finely chopped coriander (cilantro) stalks

250 g (9 oz) broccolini, end of stalks removed and discarded

1 small handful mint, roughly chopped

Heat a small pot with the kombu water, 1 teaspoon of grated ginger, the garlic, 1 teaspoon of the ground wakame and tamari. Bring to the boil, then reduce the heat and simmer gently.

Preheat the oven to 200°C (400°F). Cut a piece of baking paper about half the size of an A4 page, or preheat your air fryer to 170°C (325°F).

Lay the fish fillet in the middle of the baking paper. Season the fish with a pinch of salt and pepper and add a little squeeze of lemon.

Sprinkle the fillet with the ½ teaspoon of ginger and the chopped coriander stalks. Slice the lemon into thin slices and lay over the top of the fish. Wrap the fish up loosely with the baking paper. Place the fish parcel onto a small baking tray. Cook the fish for 8–10 minutes in the oven or in the air fryer until the flesh of the fish just flakes away when gently touched with a fork. Set the fish aside.

Plunge the broccolini into the simmering kombu broth and blanch for 1 minute, then remove immediately from the water and place onto the serving plates.

Sprinkle the broccolini with some salt and pepper, the remaining ground wakame and some of the kombu broth. Lay the fish on top of the vegetables. Top the fish with the fresh mint and serve with the extra wedge of lemon.

Moroccan roasted cauliflower with grilled fish

Spices make such an impact on this dish, with one of my favourite combinations, Ras el hanout or my Moroccan spice blend (page 40), lending such a wonderfully uplifting hand to the cauliflower.

140 g (5 oz) raw cauliflower florets

Himalayan salt and freshly ground black pepper

2 teaspoons Moroccan spice blend (page 42)

1 tablespoon ground wakame (page 40)

1 teaspoon finely chopped flat-leaf (Italian) parsley

125 g (4½ oz) piece of white fish fillet

½ lime, zested and juiced

1 small handful mint, coriander (cilantro) or basil leaves

1 lime wedge, to serve

Preheat the oven to 200°C (400°F) and line a small roasting tray with baking paper.

Place the cauliflower florets in a small pot and just cover with water. Add a pinch of salt and bring the pot to the boil. Allow the cauliflower to cook for 5 minutes, then drain the cauliflower.

Pat the cauliflower dry with a paper towel, then sprinkle with the Moroccan spice blend, half the ground wakame and the finely chopped parsley. Season with a little salt and pepper and lay the cauliflower in a single layer on the roasting tray, leaving space for the fish.

Pat the fish fillet dry with a paper towel, drizzle with the lime juice and sprinkle over the zest. Top with the rest of the ground wakame and season with salt and pepper.

Place the fish onto the roasting tray alongside the cauliflower and cook in the oven for 8–10 minutes, or until the cauliflower is tender and the fish is just cooked through. The fish should flake easily when gently touched with a fork.

Serve the cauliflower and fish topped with fresh herbs and a lime wedge on the side.

Spicy prawns with pesto zucchini

For those who like it a little hot, this dish was designed with you in mind. Using my extra special sugar-free and oil-free chilli sauce, you can turn the heat up on these prawns a little or a lot.

1 tablespoon Bridget's sticky sauce (page 25)

1 tablespoon happy hot sauce (page 38)

150 g (5½ oz) raw prawn (shrimp) tails

300 g (10½ oz) zucchini (courgette), peeled into noodles

1 tablespoon ground wakame (page 40)

3 tablespoons oil-free pesto (page 26)

Himalayan salt and freshly ground black pepper

1 small handful baby basil leaves

Combine the sticky sauce and the hot sauce. Coat the prawns with the sauces, making sure they are well covered. You could leave the prawns to marinate for 30–60 minutes to allow the flavours time to develop (or you can even freeze your prawns at this stage, to defrost when you are ready to cook and eat them).

Heat a wok or large frying pan over medium–high heat with the tamari and add the prawns. Cook the prawns, stirring often, for 60–90 seconds, then remove the prawns from the pan.

Placing the pan back over the heat, add the zucchini noodles and pesto. Toss and stir-fry very quickly, for no longer than 30 seconds.

Season the noodles and place them in a plate topped with the prawns, wakame and baby basil leaves.

Roasted garlic prawns with Asian greens

Aside from the fact that this dish is incredibly quick to make, it's also a lovely light, clean meal that uses sweet, tasty prawns (shrimp) and lightly cooked Asian green vegetables. It's my go-to meal when I'm in a rush but still want the lightness and brightness of good healthy food.

300 ml (10½ fl oz) kombu water (page 34)

1 tablespoon low-sodium tamari

1 tablespoon grated ginger

150 g (5½ oz) raw prawn (shrimp) tails

2 teaspoons finely chopped garlic

1 teaspoon lemon zest

Himalayan salt and freshly ground black pepper

170 g (6 oz) baby bok choy (pak choy), washed with outer leaves removed and discarded

2 teaspoons finely chopped coriander (cilantro) stalks

¼ sheet nori, finely sliced into very thin strips

Preheat the oven to 200°C (400°F) and line a small roasting tray with baking paper, or preheat an air fryer to 180°C (350°F).

In a pot, bring the kombu water, tamari and ginger to a gentle simmer.

Place the prawn tails on the roasting tray, sprinkle with the garlic, lemon zest and season with salt and pepper. Cook the prawns for 6—8 minutes, or until the prawns are just cooked. They should go from being translucent to being a pale orange colour.

If using an air fryer, place the seasoned prawns into the air fryer basket and cook for 6—7 minutes, or until the prawns go from being translucent to being a pale orange colour.

Add the bok choy to the simmering broth and cook for 30—60 seconds, or until the vegetables are just tender but still a vibrant green colour.

Remove the vegetables from the pot and place in a deep bowl. Spoon over some of the kombu broth. Top with the roasted prawns and garlic. Sprinkle with the coriander stalks and season with a little salt and pepper. Finish the dish with a nest of the finely sliced nori.

TIP You can use any type of Asian green you fancy in this recipe with my personal favourites including bok choy, choy sum and pak choy.

TIP Keep the kombu water that you use to blanch the greens. Allow the kombu water to cool, then store in the fridge to use in another recipe.

Sticky fish on a red cabbage slaw

Add the word sticky to any type of food and you have me hooked. The same can be said for this sticky fish recipe, as it's a glorious way to enjoy a tender white fish fillet.

125 g (4½ oz) white fish fillet

Himalayan salt and freshly ground black pepper

1 tablespoon Bridget's sticky sauce (page 25)

100 g (3½ oz) red cabbage, very finely sliced

½ green apple, sliced into matchsticks

1 small handful finely shredded mint

1 small handful finely shredded coriander (cilantro)

2 tablespoons Bridget's zesty dressing (page 28)

1 tablespoon happy hot sauce (optional) (page 38)

1 lemon or lime wedge, to serve

Preheat the grill (broiler) to high and line a small roasting tray with baking paper.

For the air fryer, preheat for 2 minutes to 160°C (315°F) and lay a small piece of baking paper in the basket.

Season the fish with salt and pepper and rub the sticky sauce over the surface.

If using the oven, place the fish onto the roasting tray and cook for 8–10 minutes.

If using the air fryer, place the fish in the air fryer and cook for 8–10 minutes, or until just cooked.

While the fish cooks, make the slaw by mixing together the cabbage, apple, mint and coriander. Season well with salt and pepper and stir through the zesty dressing. Add a little of the happy hot sauce if using and taste for flavour, adding more seasoning or zesty dressing according to your preference.

Serve the slaw alongside the sticky fish and a wedge of lemon or lime.

TIP I cooked my fish in an air fryer, but you can still get great results if you cook your fish under the grill or broiler. I've given instructions for both methods.

Steamed mussels with kombu kale

Fresh mussels, still nestled in their shell, are a wonderful treat. They are juicy and taste of the sea, and when combined with this simple kombu broth, they are a satisfying meal.

200 ml (7 fl oz) kombu water (page 34)

1 tablespoon finely chopped ginger

1 teaspoon finely chopped garlic

2 tablespoons ground wakame (page 40)

150 g (5½ oz) raw mussel meat, still in the shell

2 large handfuls of fresh kale leaves, stripped from the stalks

1 teaspoon cumin powder

Himalayan salt and freshly ground black pepper

1 teaspoon chopped flat-leaf (Italian) parsley

1 teaspoon chopped basil

½ red chilli, finely chopped

Heat the kombu water, ginger, garlic and half the wakame in a large pot until it simmers. Add the mussels and cover with a lid. Allow the mussels to steam and as soon as the shells open, remove the mussels and set aside. Cook until all the mussel shells open, discarding any that have not opened.

Add the kale to the kombu broth along with the cumin powder and cook for 30 seconds (no longer!).

Remove the kale from the pot and add to a plate. Season with salt and pepper, then add the mussels to the noodles and pour over some of the broth.

Sprinkle the mussels with the remaining wakame, parsley, basil and chilli and serve.

TIP If you can buy fresh mussels, still in the shell, this dish will be heavenly. As the mussels cook and the shells open, they release their juices that will combine to make a wonderful sauce.

TIP In order to weigh the raw mussel meat, open one raw mussel and weigh the meat (not the shell!) and then you can work out approximately how many mussels you will need to cook to equal the weight stated in the ingredients list.

Charred squid and asparagus salad

Lightly cooked and tender, charred baby squid makes for a delightful salad.

125 g (4½ oz) baby squid, defrosted if frozen

1 tablespoon Bridget's sticky sauce (page 25)

1 teaspoon finely chopped red chilli (optional)

½ lime, zested and juiced, plus 1 lime wedge to serve

Himalayan salt and freshly ground black pepper

200 g (7 oz) asparagus, approximately 15–20 stalks

2 tablespoons oil-free pesto (page 26)

1 small handful baby basil, mint or coriander (cilantro), to serve

Preheat your barbecue to high (if using).

Cut the baby squid into strips, or if feeling adventurous, slice the squid open and using a very sharp knife lightly score the flesh of the squid in a criss-cross fashion.

Rub the squid all over with the sticky sauce, chilli and lime juice and season with salt and pepper.

Prepare the asparagus by snapping the ends of the asparagus stalks off and discarding. Where the asparagus naturally breaks is the woody part that is not very nice to eat. Discard the woody ends. Drizzle the oil-free pesto over the asparagus and roll the asparagus to ensure even coating.

If using a frying pan for this recipe, heat a large heavy-based pan over high heat and add 1 teaspoon of tamari. Add the asparagus and cook for 1–1½ minutes, turning the asparagus often to ensure even cooking. Remove the asparagus from the pan and add the squid. Cook for 1 minute, stirring the squid often to get even cooking.

If using the barbecue, add the asparagus and the squid to the barbecue and cook for 1–1½ minutes, or until just done.

Place the asparagus on a plate and sprinkle with salt and pepper and the lime zest. Add the squid and herbs and serve with the lime wedge.

TIP It's a great (and easy) idea to buy your squid frozen, then defrost by allowing to sit in cold water for 10 minutes.

Stir-fried curried mussels and zucchini ribbons

An exceptionally quick and tasty mussel stir-fry with tender, sweet zucchini.

200 ml (7 fl oz) saffron water (page 33)

¾ teaspoon turmeric powder

2 teaspoons curry powder

1 teaspoon lemon zest

2 teaspoons ground wakame (page 40)

150 g (5½ oz) raw mussel meat, finely diced

300 g (10½ oz) zucchini (courgette), sliced or peeled into ribbons

Himalayan salt and freshly ground black pepper

2 tablespoons finely chopped coriander (cilantro), basil or fenugreek leaves

1 lemon wedge, to serve

Heat a non-stick wok or large frying pan over medium–high heat with the saffron water, turmeric, curry powder, lemon zest and wakame. Bring to a simmer and allow to gently heat for 3–4 minutes to allow the sauce time to reduce a little to concentrate the flavour.

Add the mussel meat and cook for 10 seconds, then toss in the zucchini ribbons and stir. Cook for another 30 seconds, then remove the pan from the heat and season well with salt and pepper.

Toss the herbs through and serve, pouring over the liquid and finishing with a slice of lemon.

TIP Choose raw mussel meat for this recipe and cook quickly for optimum results! Most seafood only requires the lightest heat to cook through.

Parcel-baked fish with cauliflower steak

Baking fish in a small parcel is a fantastic way to lock in all the moisture in your fish fillet. You can also add flavours to your parcel that will permeate the fish as it gently cooks.

140 g (5 oz) slice of raw cauliflower

2 tablespoons oil-free pesto (page 26)

1 teaspoon cumin powder

1 teaspoon garam masala

1 teaspoon thyme leaves

Himalayan salt and freshly ground black pepper

125 g (4½ oz) white fish fillet or 100 g (3½ oz) salmon fillet

½ lemon, juiced

1 teaspoon finely chopped coriander (cilantro)

Preheat the oven to 200°C (400°F) and line a small roasting tray with baking paper.

Lay the cauliflower on the tray and drizzle with 1 tablespoon of the oil-free pesto. Sprinkle over the cumin, garam masala and thyme leaves. Season with salt and pepper. Cook the cauliflower slice for 20 minutes.

While the cauliflower cooks, cut a piece of baking paper about half the size of an A4 page. Lay the fish in the middle of the paper and drizzle over the lemon juice. Add the coriander stalks and season with salt and pepper. Wrap the fish loosely to make a parcel, then place in the oven alongside the cauliflower slice.

Bake the fish for 8–10 minutes, or until just cooked. The fish should easily flake when gently touched with a fork.

When the cauliflower is tender, serve on a plate with the fish and any juices from the parcel poured over the top. Drizzle with 1 tablespoon of the oil-free pesto and serve with a little salt and pepper over the top.

Oven-baked fish with broccoli chips

Crisp and crunchy, broccoli chips baked with garlic and my oil-free pesto are a delightful way to enjoy all that green goodness. This dish is a one pan special, so cleaning up is left to a minimum!

125 g (4½ oz) white fish fillet or 100 g (3½ oz) salmon fillet

1 teaspoon tamari and lime sauce (page 31)

1 lemon wedge, juiced

1 teaspoon grated ginger

few leaves of coriander (cilantro) and mint

Himalayan salt and freshly ground black pepper

250 g (9 oz) raw broccoli florets

2 teaspoons finely chopped garlic

2 tablespoons oil-free pesto (page 26)

1 tablespoon ground wakame (page 40)

Preheat the oven to 200°C (400°F) and line a small roasting tray with baking paper.

Cut a piece of baking paper about half the size of an A4 page and lay the fish fillet in the middle of the paper. Drizzle the tamari sauce over the fish followed by the lemon juice, the grated ginger, herbs and a bit of salt and pepper. Lightly wrap the fish like a small parcel.

In a mixing bowl, stir the broccoli with the chopped garlic, oil-free pesto, ground wakame and season well with salt and pepper. Lay the broccoli on the roasting tray in a single layer and cook in the oven for 15–20 minutes, or until tender.

Halfway through the broccoli cooking time, add the fish parcel and cook the fish alongside the broccoli for 8–10 minutes, or until the fish is just cooked.

Serve the broccoli next to the fish, making sure to pour the juices from the parcel over the broccoli as well.

Air fryer fish with kombu asparagus

Using a kombu broth is such a lovely way to cook asparagus . If you don't own an air fryer, don't worry! You can make this recipe using a frying pan as well and I have given methods for both.

15–20 asparagus spears, snapped at the base

250 ml (9 fl oz/1 cup) kombu water (page 34)

1 tablespoon grated ginger

1 teaspoon finely chopped garlic

125 g (4½ oz) white fish fillet or 100 g (3½ oz) salmon fillet

2 tablespoons Bridget's sticky sauce (page 25)

2 teaspoons ground wakame (page 40)

Himalayan salt and freshly ground black pepper

1 small handful chopped mint

1 lemon wedge, to serve

In a large non-stick wok, heat the kombu water, 1 tablespoon of sticky sauce, the grated ginger and the chopped garlic until it comes to a simmer.

Preheat the air fryer for 2 minutes to 160°C (315°F), or if using a frying pan, heat the pan over medium heat and lay a piece of baking paper in the pan.

Rub the remaining sticky sauce into the fish fillet and sprinkle over 1 teaspoon of ground wakame. Season with salt and pepper and place the fish into the air fryer or the pan and cook for 6–8 minutes, or until the fish is just cooked.

While the fish cooks, add the asparagus to the kombu water. Cook for 1 minute, or until the asparagus is just tender but still a vibrant green colour.

Remove the vegetables from the kombu broth and add them to a bowl. Place the cooked fish on top and pour over some of the broth. Season the dish with salt and pepper, ground wakame, chopped mint and serve with a lemon wedge.

TIP Don't discard any leftover kombu broth, as it keeps well when stored in the refrigerator and you can use it to steam other vegetables, poach fish, or create a base for soup or curries.

Fish pie

I grew up with fish pie, but not the healthy version like we have here! I top this pie with a creamy cauliflower mash and make the base with a little curry powder, fresh herbs and wakame to add flavour.

125 g (4½ oz) firm white fish fillet, diced into small pieces

200 ml (7 fl oz) kombu water (page 34)

2 tablespoons ground wakame (page 40)

1 tablespoon tamari and lime sauce (page 31)

2 teaspoons curry powder

1 tablespoon chopped chives

1 tablespoon chopped flat-leaf (Italian) parsley

140 g (5 oz) cauliflower florets

Himalayan salt and freshly ground black pepper

1 teaspoon finely chopped rosemary leaves

2 roasted garlic cloves, mashed

¼ teaspoon nutmeg

¼ teaspoon cumin

To make the fish stew for the base of the pie, heat the kombu water with the ground wakame, tamari dressing, and curry powder. Once it comes to a simmer, add the fish and bring to a gentle boil.

Cook the fish for 4–5 minutes, or until tender and the broth has reduced a little and the flavour has concentrated. Taste the broth, adding salt and pepper to taste along with the chives and parsley.

For the cauliflower topping, place the cauliflower florets in pot with just enough water to cover and season with a pinch of salt. Bring the water to the boil, then turn down the heat until the water is rapidly simmering. Cook the cauliflower for 12–15 minutes, or until very tender.

Drain the water from the cauliflower well. This step is very important to help make sure you get a smooth cauliflower mash or purée rather than a watery one. Shake the cauliflower well to ensure all the water is drained.

Blend the cauliflower until very smooth using a small, fast food processor or a stick blender. Add the rosemary leaves, roasted garlic, nutmeg and cumin and season to taste with a little salt and pepper and blend to mix through the mash.

Add the fish stew to a small casserole or ovenproof dish and top with the cauliflower mash. Smooth out the cauliflower and place the dish under a hot grill (broiler) until warmed and lightly browned on top.

TIP This dish is great to make if you are able to get your hands on a firm white fish like monk or ling, as the fish holds together really well and makes a nice base for your pie. Ask your fishmonger if in doubt!

Bok choy broth with clams

Clams or pipis hold fond memories of weekends spent at the beach with toes stuck in the sand, foraging for baskets of shellfish. I adore the freshness and sweet ocean flavour that fresh shellfish affords and its combination here with tender bok choy (pak choy) is just perfect.

150 g (5½ oz) cockle, clam or pipi meat, still in the shell

100 ml (3½ fl oz) kombu water (page 34)

1 tablespoon low-sodium tamari

1 tablespoon grated ginger

1 teaspoon crushed garlic

250 g (9 oz) baby bok choy (pak choy), tough outer leaves removed and discarded

Himalayan salt and freshly ground black pepper

1 tablespoon oil-free pesto (page 26)

1 tablespoon chopped coriander (cilantro) or basil leaves

1 tablespoon chopped chives

Heat a large frying pan or wok over medium–high heat and add the cockles. Place a lid over the cockles. Reduce the heat to medium and allow the cockles to continue to steam open, removing each cockle as soon as the shell springs open. Set the cockle aside in a bowl.

There should be about 125 ml (4 fl oz/½ cup) of natural liquid in the base of the pan which is full of flavour so don't discard this! Add the kombu water, tamari, ginger and garlic to the pan and heat until simmering.

Add the bok choy to the liquid and cook for 30–60 seconds, or until the vegetables are just tender.

Place the bok choy at the bottom of a deep bowl, and season with a little salt and pepper. Add the cockles on top of the bok choy, then pour the liquid from the pan over the top of the cockles until it creates a little pool of liquid in the plate.

Drizzle the oil-free pesto into the cockle shells. Sprinkle over the coriander leaves and chives and season with a little salt and pepper before serving.

TIP I use New Zealand little neck clams or cockles as they are called but you can also use pipis or vongole. The best way to measure how many clams you will need is to weigh one, flesh only, which should give you an accurate estimate of how many you will need to make up 150 g (5½ oz) of meat. I calculated 4–5 g (⅛ oz) per clam, so I used 30 little clams.

Poached fish with garlic and ginger bok choy

Fresh garlic and ginger has such an affinity with bok choy (pak choy). Combined here with sticky sauce and lightly poached fish, you have a majestic meal.

200 ml (7 oz) kombu water (page 34)

1 tablespoon Bridget's sticky sauce (page 25)

1 teaspoon crushed garlic

125 g (4½ oz) white fish fillet

250 g (9 oz) baby bok choy (pak choy), tough outer leaves removed and discarded

Himalayan salt and freshly ground black pepper

1 tablespoon grated ginger

2 teaspoons finely chopped chives

Heat a large frying pan or wok over medium–high heat with the kombu water, half of the sticky sauce and the garlic until simmering.

Carefully slide the fish fillet into the simmering broth and cook for 3–4 minutes, or until the fillet is just cooked. Using a wide spatula, remove the fish from the broth and set aside.

Add the baby bok choy to the broth and allow it to cook for 30–60 seconds, or until the vegetables are tender but still vibrant and green.

Remove the bok choy from the water and place it in a bowl alongside the fish and cover with foil to keep warm.

Heat the liquid in the pan over high heat and allow it to boil and reduce a little to create a flavoursome broth. Taste for flavour and add a little salt and pepper if required. Pour this broth over top of the vegetables and scatter the ginger over the bok choy, along with the last of the sticky sauce right over the vegetables.

Season again with salt and pepper and finish with chopped chives before serving.

One pan chicken and asparagus

This recipe is so simple and quick, yet the results are marvellous. The chicken is cooked in a small parcel so you lock in the moisture and the vegetables are flashed quickly in the oven so they remain crunchy yet tender. Everything is cooked on the baking tray, making cleaning up simple too.

100 g (3½ oz) raw chicken or turkey breast, skin removed

Himalayan salt and freshly ground black pepper

1 teaspoon lemon zest

3 teaspoons oil-free pesto (page 26)

3 large leaves basil, finely sliced

5 coriander (cilantro) leaves

300 g (10½ oz) asparagus

2 teaspoons ground wakame (page 40)

Preheat the oven to 190°C (375°F).

Slice the chicken breast into 4–5 even-sized slices and lay onto a large square of baking paper. Season the chicken with salt and pepper. Sprinkle over the lemon zest, 1 teaspoon of the oil-free pesto and half of the sliced basil. Wrap the chicken into a little parcel and place on a baking tray.

Break the base of the asparagus stalks off where they snap, discard the woody ends. Lay the spear ends of the asparagus on to the tray, ensuring they are in a single layer.

Season the asparagus with salt and pepper, and dribble over a couple of teaspoons of the basil and lemon pesto. Add the remaining sliced basil and sprinkle over the ground wakame.

Place the tray in the oven and bake for 8–12 minutes, or until the chicken is cooked through and tender and the asparagus is also tender.

Serve the chicken on top of the asparagus and drizzle any liquid from the parcel over the top of the chicken. Enjoy!

TIP There is nothing like homemade pesto, and the sauce that I use in this recipe is fresh and crisp in flavour. Using fresh sweet basil, lemon to balance and garlic to mellow, it is a great sauce to keep on hand for using on salads, vegetables and meats.

Teriyaki-style chicken and slaw

This, in my mind, is one of those incredibly simple meal prep dishes. The chicken is soaked overnight, or even frozen in sticky sauce, then cooked quickly and effortlessly the next day.

500 g (1 lb 2 oz) raw chicken breast, skin removed and chicken sliced thinly

120 ml (4¼ fl oz) Bridget's sticky sauce (page 25)

2 tablespoons fibre syrup (optional)

700 g (1 lb 9 oz) white cabbage, very thinly sliced

1 large handful mint leaves, finely chopped

1 large handful coriander (cilantro) or basil leaves, finely chopped

Himalayan salt and freshly ground black pepper

5 tablespoons apple cider vinegar

2 tablespoons inulin powder

½ teaspoon freshly grated ginger

¼ sheet nori, folded and very finely sliced into thin strands

5 teaspoons white sesame seeds (optional)

Place the chicken into a large zip lock bag and add the sticky sauce and fibre syrup. Press the sauce all over the chicken in the bag and place the bag in the fridge overnight to give the flavours time to marinate deeply into the flesh.

When you're ready to cook the chicken, heat an air fryer to 200°C (400°F) or preheat the oven on 220°C (425°F).

Place the chicken in a single layer in the air fryer and cook for 7–8 minutes, or until well cooked and caramelised. It is important to not overcrowd your air fryer. This will help achieve the beautiful colour and crisp exterior.

If you are using an oven, place the chicken on a roasting tray lined with baking paper. Cook for 7–10 minutes, or until cooked through. While the chicken cooks, make the coleslaw by mixing together the cabbage, mint and coriander and season with a little salt and pepper.

Make the dressing by mixing together the apple cider vinegar, inulin powder and ginger. Taste the dressing for flavour, adding more inulin if necessary.

Plate up the chicken, add a handful of the slaw and drizzle over some of the dressing. Sprinkle with the nori and sesame seeds and serve!

TIP Fibre syrup helps give the chicken its caramelised colour. It is the syrup equivalent of inulin powder and a great alternative to honey, maple and agave. You can purchase fibre syrup online (the brand I use is Sukrin).

Honey (less) mustard chicken

This is such a well-known dish that I didn't want to take away from the much-loved original. I received a request to make a healthy version of this dish, otherwise I may never have tested it out. I was pleasantly surprised by how close to the original flavour I was able to achieve with this recipe; it's not overly sweet but rather full and robust yet well balanced and flavoursome.

2 large green apples, peeled and diced

2 kg (4 lb 8 oz) skinless chicken thighs, trimmed of excess fat (or you can use chicken breast)

4 tablespoons dijon mustard (sugar and gluten-free variety, I use Maille dijon mustard)

4 tablespoons clear fibre syrup (page 18) (optional)

1 tablespoon low-sodium tamari

120 ml (4 fl oz) kombu water (page 34)

1 tablespoon finely chopped garlic

½ teaspoon turmeric powder

Himalayan salt and freshly ground black pepper

2 tablespoons finely chopped basil or mint, to serve

Add 200 ml (7 fl oz) of water to a small pot along with the apple. Bring the pot to the boil and cook the apple for 10–15 minutes, or until tender. Drain the water from the apple well, then purée in a small food processor until smooth.

Add the chicken, dijon mustard, fibre syrup, tamari, kombu water, garlic, turmeric powder and 120 g (4¼ oz) of the puréed apple to the pressure or slow cooker. Stir to combine and season with a little salt and pepper.

If using a pressure cooker, set the cooker to high and pressure cook for 15 minutes. If using a slow cooker, set the cooker to high for 4 hours or low for 6–8 hours. The chicken should be fall-apart tender when it's ready.

Carefully remove the chicken from the cooker and keep the chicken warm by covering with a lid or foil.

Pour the sauce from the cooker into a large pot and set this pot over high heat. Boil the sauce until it reduces down and thickens a little to be more gravy-like in consistency. Taste this sauce for flavour, adding more salt and pepper if required. Pour the hot sauce over the chicken and sprinkle with the herbs. Serve with your favourite vegetables!

TIP Serve this chicken dish with lightly blanched asparagus or broccoli or for a lighter option, a fresh green salad.

Steamed chicken and Asian greens

The spices in this recipe work well with chicken without being overpowering. The result is tender and flavourful. The vegetables can be steamed in the same pot.

100 g (3½ oz) raw chicken or turkey fillets (tenderloins) or chicken breast, skin removed

1 teaspoon allspice

1 teaspoon Chinese five-spice

2 tablespoons ground wakame (page 40)

3 tablespoons tamari and lime sauce (page 31), heated gently in the microwave or on the stovetop

250 g (9 oz) bok choy (pak choy)

1 teaspoon mustard seeds, lightly toasted

Himalayan salt and freshly ground black pepper

1 small handful basil leaves

1 small handful coriander (cilantro) leaves

Sprinkle the chicken fillets with the allspice and five-spice and rub into the meat, distributing the spices well. Sprinkle over 1 tablespoon of the ground wakame and leave to develop the flavours for 30–60 minutes, if you have the time.

Prepare the vegetables by discarding the thick outer leaves of the bok choy to reveal the tender leaves.

Prepare the pot for steaming, or your steamer equipment as per manufacturer's instructions. If using a pot, add 15 cm (6 in) of warm water to a large pot and place the steamer basket on top of the pot. Add a well-fitted lid and set the pot over medium–high heat. Allow the steam to build up in the basket.

Place the chicken fillets into the steamer and steam for 8–12 minutes, or until the chicken is cooked through but still juicy. Keep an eye on the fillets, testing to see if they are cooked through.

Remove the fillets from the basket and set aside. Add the greens to the basket, replace the lid, and steam the vegetables for 3–5 minutes, or until just steamed through and the bok choy is a little crunchy.

To serve, place the greens on a deep plate and top with some of the chicken fillets. Sprinkle over the additional 1 tablespoon of ground wakame and mustard seeds and season well with salt and pepper. Top with the herbs and pour over some of the warm tamari dressing to form a pool at the base of the plate for dipping your vegetables and chicken into.

Lemon garlic chicken

This dish is reminiscent of my childhood, except I've turned up the garlic quota! You can make this all sticky with my sauce, then stir-fry it quickly with your favourite green vegetable. I've chosen broccoli for my mean green vegetable.

2 tablespoons Bridget's sticky sauce (page 25)

1 lemon, juiced

1 tablespoon finely chopped garlic

100 g (3½ oz) raw chicken breast, thinly sliced

300 g (10½ oz) broccoli florets, cut into small bite-sized florets (you could also use asparagus or cabbage)

Himalayan salt and freshly ground black pepper

1 small handful baby basil and mint leaves

1 teaspoon ground wakame (page 40)

Heat a large frying pan or wok over medium–high heat. Add the sticky sauce, lemon juice and garlic and stir-fry for 30 seconds.

Add the chicken breast and stir-fry for a 2–3 minutes. Add the broccoli to the pan along with 120 ml (4 fl oz) of water and stir-fry for a few more minutes.

Season the dish with salt and pepper and taste the sauce for flavour, adding more seasoning to taste. Serve topped with the herbs and sprinkled with ground wakame.

Broccoli and chicken soup

Oh baby, it's cold outside! As soon as the weather turns chilly, I'm instantly drawn to the kitchen where I want to create a soothing hot soup and this recipe is very easy to make and serve.

600 ml (21 fl oz) kombu water (page 34)

2 tablespoons low-sodium tamari

1 teaspoon Himalayan salt

3 garlic cloves, crushed

1 tablespoon freshly grated ginger

180 g (6½ oz) cooked chicken breast, shredded

400 g (14 oz) raw broccoli florets, sliced into small, even pieces

3 tablespoons chopped coriander (cilantro) and flat-leaf (Italian) parsley leaves

1 tablespoon chopped coriander (cilantro) root

1 tablespoon ground wakame (page 40)

freshly ground black pepper

Heat the kombu water in a pot over medium–high heat. Add the tamari, salt, garlic and ginger, and taste for flavour. The broth should taste light and fresh.

Bring to a simmer, then add the chicken and broccoli and gently heat for 5 minutes. Add the chopped herbs and coriander root and stir through. Taste the soup for flavour, adding more seasoning if required.

Sprinkle over the ground wakame and serve.

TIP You could use cooked turkey breast here, or replace the chicken with tofu for a vegetarian version.

Cauliflower chicken nuggets

If you are in search of a different type of coating for chicken, fish or prawns, look no further than this cauliflower crust. Yes, I said cauliflower!

100 g (3½ oz) raw cauliflower

30 g (1 oz) desiccated coconut (optional)

1 tablespoon psyllium husk

Himalayan salt and freshly ground black pepper

200 g (7 oz) raw chicken breast, cut into bite-sized chunks and soaked in water to cover

2 lemon wedges, to serve

Place the cauliflower in a food processor or blender and blitz for a couple of seconds, or until it resembles the texture of rice.

If using the coconut, mix through the cauliflower rice along with the psyllium husk and season with salt and pepper.

Once the chicken has been soaking for a couple of minutes, drain the water and taking a piece of chicken at a time, press into the crumb mixture.

Preheat the air fryer to 200°C (400°F). Place the chicken nuggets into the air fryer basket and cook for 6–8 minutes, or until the nuggets are golden and the chicken is cooked through.

If you are using the oven, preheat the oven to 200°C (400°F) and line a baking tray with baking paper. Place the nuggets on the tray and cook for 15 minutes.

Serve the nuggets alongside your favourite vegetables, with a salad, or simply with lemon wedges.

TIP I used an air fryer for this recipe. You can also make the nuggets in the oven but they won't turn out quite as crisp and golden.

TIP Serve these nuggets with cauliflower rice (page 256) or zucchini chips (page 264).

HEALTHY TREATS.

When you start living a healthier lifestyle it isn't necessary for those cakes, crumbles, pies and delicious desserts to become a distant memory.

If you love the comforting flavours and textures of old-fashioned treats, try my healthy alternatives knowing that you won't be compromising your health goals.

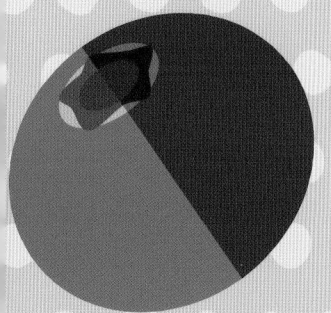

Treats

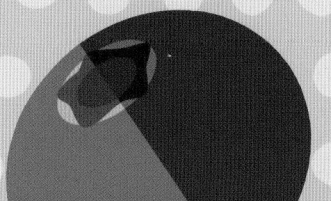

Dairy-, gluten- and sugar-free vegan dark chocolate

From struggle comes invention - such was the case with this recipe. After struggling for months and months, trying to find affordable sugar- and dairy-free chocolate in my local supermarkets or stores, the time came to find an alternative that was easier to source and simple to make. Step aside, store-bought dark chocolate. We can now make our own and it's easier to make than falling off a log.

50 g (1¾ oz) pure cacao butter buttons or pieces

3 tablespoons raw cacao powder

2–3 tablespoons inulin powder

In a small saucepan over medium to low heat, melt the cacao butter until liquid. This will only take a couple of minutes.

Stir in the cacao and inulin powder and add one of the flavour variations in the below list (if using).

Pour the chocolate into silicone chocolate moulds, or spread out onto a small roasting tray or sandwich tin lined with non-stick baking paper. Place the chocolate moulds or tin in the freezer for 10 minutes to set.

Turn the hardened chocolate out of the moulds or break into small pieces. You will need to store the chocolate in an airtight container in the fridge to stop it from melting. Store for up to 4 weeks.

Variations
Add any of the following flavourings or a combo of your favourites.

½ teaspoon pure vanilla extract

2 tablespoons finely chopped almonds, hazelnuts, pecans, pistachios or walnuts

2 tablespoons roughly chopped goji berries

¼–½ teaspoon pure peppermint oil

2 tablespoons dried rose petals, roughly broken up

2 tablespoons desiccated coconut, raw or lightly toasted

continued overleaf

Dairy-, gluten- and sugar-free vegan dark chocolate

2 tablespoons cacao nibs

2 tablespoons finely chopped dried unsweetened cherries, blueberries or cranberries

½ tablespoon finely zested orange or mandarin

Sprinkle of sea salt flakes (added on top of the warm chocolate after pouring into the moulds)

1 tablespoon bee pollen *(this variation is not vegan)*

2 tablespoons chopped freeze-dried strawberries

Use this chocolate for your chocolate chips in baking, grate it over cakes and coconut yoghurt, melt it through your favourite non-dairy milk for hot chocolate, or have it as a healthy nibble alternative.

NOTE This recipe uses inulin powder. This is a dietary fibre and prebiotic, so excessive consumption of this chocolate may have a laxative effect. Remember, a little goes a long way!

TIP You will need to source cacao butter for this recipe, which you can find online or at a good health food store. Cacao butter is extracted from the cacao bean and is the base for all chocolate-making. Cacao butter looks like white chocolate, but has very little taste.

TIP Choose organic cacao butter and organic cacao powder, if possible, to take your chocolate to next-level amazing!

3-ingredient wobble pancakes

If you are following a gluten-, sugar- and dairy-free diet, it can be difficult to make pancakes - in fact, it can be nearly impossible. This recipe makes it possible to feel like you're indulging when you are actually eating fresh, clean and healthy.

1 large ripe banana

2 eggs

½ teaspoon ground cinnamon

Coconut oil spray, for lightly greasing the pan (optional)

Fibre syrup to serve

Separate the egg whites from the yolks and place the yolks into a small bowl or blender. Add the banana and cinnamon to the egg yolks and blend or mash, then whisk until well combined.

In a clean bowl, whisk the egg whites until they form stiff peaks, which hold their shape when the whisk is removed. Fold the whites gently through the banana mixture, as lightly as possible. If the mixture looks lumpy, that's perfectly alright!

Heat a non-stick frying pan on medium heat and spray lightly with coconut oil or, if not using oil, place a piece of non-stick baking paper into the base of the pan. To make a pancake, add 2 tablespoons of the mixture and cook for 60–90 seconds on one side, before carefully flipping and continuing to cook on the other side for a further 30–60 seconds.

Remove the pancake from the pan and continue cooking until all the batter is used.

Serve immediately with a drizzle of fibre syrup, squeeze of fresh lemon juice and sprinkle of inulin powder, or fresh berries and coconut yoghurt.

Sugar-free berry chia jam

To me, summer holidays in the top end of New Zealand - the winterless north - meant picking blackberries from out of the brambles. Skipping along dirt roads, basket in hand, surrounded by a posse of rabble-rousing cousins, we would carefully pick the blackberries off the prickly bushes, staining fingers and clothes as well as our waiting mouths. I'm not sure how many blackberries ultimately made it back to the farmhouse, but we usually had enough for dessert, which was either eaten with fresh cream and powdered sugar, or made into a jam to spread on baked flatbread.

300 g (10½ oz) fresh or frozen blackberries

60 ml (2 fl oz) water

50 g (1¾ oz) fibre syrup

20 g (¾ oz) chia seeds

Add the berries, water and fibre syrup to a food processor and pulse until just blended. Add the chia seeds and pulse once to just combine.

Spoon the mixture into a clean glass jar and seal with a tight-fitting lid. The jam is ready to use after 1 hour.

Store in the refrigerator for up to 1 month.

TIP If blackberries aren't your thing, you could try the following delicious combinations: cranberries, zest of ¼ lemon and ¼ lime, and 1 teaspoon ground cinnamon; blueberries, zest of ¼ lemon and 1 teaspoon crushed coriander seeds; mixed berries, zest of ¼ lemon and seeds scraped from ½ vanilla pod; strawberries and ½ teaspoon orange blossom syrup

TIP Chia seeds are incredibly high in protein and have the amazing ability to increase 10 times in size when soaked in water or liquid. The seed has a gelatinous quality to it when soaked and can help foods to gel and thicken naturally.

Sea-weed crackers

These crackers are my healthy snack alternative, served alongside dips, cheese or with a party platter. They require very little effort, and the results are so worth it.

100 g (3½ oz) almond flour or meal or LSA (linseed, sunflower and almond meal)

40 g (1¼ oz) chia seeds

40 g (1¼ oz) hemp seeds (hearts)

40 g (1¼ oz) linseeds (flaxseeds)

40 g (1¼ oz) chopped sunflower or pumpkin seeds

1 teaspoon fennel seeds

1 teaspoon cumin seeds

1 teaspoon Himalayan salt

120 ml (4 fl oz) kombu or filtered water

Preheat your oven on bake to 150°C (300°F).

In a small frying pan without any oil, dry-fry the fennel and cumin seeds for 1–2 minutes on medium heat until they start to pop. Keep an eye on them because you don't want them to burn.

In a mixing bowl, add the toasted seeds along with the remaining ingredients and stir with a spoon to combine. Allow the mixture to stand for 10 minutes to thicken.

Using 2 pieces of non-stick baking paper the same size as your baking tray, place the dough and onto one piece of paper, flattening a little, then place the other piece on top of the dough.

Take a rolling pin and flatten the dough out as evenly and thinly as possible. Remove the top piece of paper and carefully place the rolled dough, still on the paper, onto your baking tray. Bake in the oven for 30–35 minutes, rotating the tray a couple of times to ensure the crackers cook evenly and are golden in colour.

Remove the tray from the oven. Allow the crackers to cool before snapping them into random rustic pieces.

When the crackers are cooled completely, store them in an airtight container for up to 2 weeks.

Healthy gut gummies

Much has been written about the beneficial properties of grass-fed gelatine in our diet. This recipe is such a fun way to get something so beneficial into our bodies!

Spiced raspberry gummies

4 tea bags of roasted dandelion tea

240 ml (8 fl oz) boiling water

200 g (7 oz) frozen raspberries, defrosted

50 g (1¼ oz) fibre syrup

200 ml (7 fl oz) cold filtered water

100 g (3½ oz) grass-fed gelatine

Chamomile and rose gummies

4 tea bags good-quality pure chamomile tea

240 ml (8 fl oz) boiling water

200 ml (7 fl oz) cold filtered water

4 tablespoons rose water

50 g (1¾ oz) fibre syrup

100 g (3½ oz) grass-fed gelatine

For both gummies, first brew the tea in a cup for 10 minutes, with a lid on to keep it very hot.

For the Spiced raspberry gummies: Add the filtered water and fibre syrup to a jug and stir together. Process the raspberries in a small blender until pureed. Using a small strainer, push through the raspberry liquid with a tablespoon into the filtered water, discarding the seeds and any pulp left in the strainer. Stir mixture in jug to combine.

For the Chamomile and rose gummies: Add the filtered water, rose water and fibre syrup to a jug and stir to combine.

For both gummies, sprinkle the gelatine over the top, allow it to sit for 30 seconds then stir with a fork. Pour over the hot brewed tea, discarding the tea bags. Stir the mixture with a fork or spoon until all the gelatine is dissolved. Using your jug, pour the liquid into moulds. Allow the gummies to set in the fridge for 60–90 minutes until firm.

Pop them out of the moulds then store them in a clean airtight container in the fridge. Eat one a day for good health! If stored correctly, they will last for 2 weeks.

TIP You will need to source a good-quality grass-fed gelatine, which you should be able to find in the health section of a good supermarket or your health food store.

TIP For setting your gummies, you will need a couple of flexible ice trays or silicone or chocolate moulds.

Fat-free veggie chips

This is a healthy snack that is totally devoid of anything unhealthy! Nibble down on a crunchy mushroom, bring beetroots to life and enjoy a cinnamon-spiced pumpkin all with a delightful crunch. You can either choose to do one type of chip or, given more time, you could do all four and mix them together for a vegetable medley. The only problem is … the crunch on these chips doesn't last long, so consume as soon as they are ready.

Eggplant chips

1 medium eggplant, sliced in half

¼ teaspoon nutmeg

½ teaspoon fine Himalayan salt

Mushroom chips

200 g (7 oz) button mushrooms

¼ teaspoon porcini powder (optional)

¼ teaspoon fine Himalayan salt

Beetroot chips

250 g (9 oz) beetroot, peeled and tops removed

½ teaspoon garlic powder

½ teaspoon fine Himalayan salt

Eggplant chips: Slice the eggplant half rounds thinly on the mandolin and place into a bowl. Sprinkle with nutmeg and salt, and mix with your fingers to distribute the seasoning evenly.

Preheat the air fryer for 2 minutes on 160°C (320°F) and add the slices to the basket. Depending on the size of your air fryer, you may need to cook the chips in batches. Cook for 10–12 minutes until crisp, tossing the chips every couple of minutes.

Mushroom chips: Slice the mushrooms a little thicker than the other chips, using the mandolin, and place the slices into a bowl. Sprinkle with porcini powder (if using) and salt, and mix with your fingers to distribute the seasoning evenly.

Preheat the air fryer for 2 minutes on 160°C (320°F) and add the slices to the basket. Depending on the size of your air fryer, you may need to cook the chips in batches. Cook for 10–12 minutes until crisp, tossing the chips every couple of minutes.

Beetroot chips: Using gloves to keep your hands and nails free from beetroot stains, slice off the top of the beetroot. Slice the beetroot into thin slices using a mandolin and place into a metal bowl. Sprinkle the beetroot with garlic powder and salt.

Preheat the air fryer for 2 minutes on 160°C (320°F) and add the slices to the basket. Depending on the size of your air fryer, you may need to cook the chips in batches. Cook for 15–18 minutes until crisp, tossing the chips every 5 minutes.

continued overleaf

Fat-free veggie chips

Pumpkin or parsnip chips

200 g (7 oz) piece of pumpkin, peeled and deseeded

¼ teaspoon ground cinnamon

¼ teaspoon mixed spice

¼ teaspoon fine Himalayan salt

Pumpkin or parsnip chips: Slice the pumpkin or parsnips thinly on the mandolin and place into a bowl. Sprinkle with cinnamon, mixed spice and salt, and mix with your fingers to distribute the seasoning evenly.

Preheat the air fryer for 2 minutes on 160°C (320°F) and add the slices to the basket. Depending on the size of your air fryer, you may need to cook the chips in batches. Cook for 15–18 minutes until crisp, tossing the chips every couple of minutes.

You can either serve these separately or mix them in a large bowl for sharing. Eat immediately, or soon after cooking, for optimum crispness.

TIP To make thin, even slices of vegetables, I used a Benriner Japanese mandolin slicer (page 19).

TIP You will also need an air fryer for the recipe.

Super-quick avocado bread

You are going to love this simple quick bread! Made with only a few ingredients and cooked in the microwave, this bread is perfect to use as a sandwich base or burger buns, under poached eggs, or to serve with soups.

1 tablespoon ripe avocado flesh

1 egg

1 heaped tablespoon of almond flour or meal or LSA (linseed, sunflower and almond meal)

¼ teaspoon baking powder

½ teaspoon psyllium husks

pinch of salt

Place all the ingredients in a small food processor and blend until smooth and well mixed.

Spoon the mixture into a small rectangular or square plastic container. Flatten and even out the mixture.

Microwave on high for 90 seconds, cook for 3—4 minutes in a pie-maker, or bake in a muffin tray lined with paper cases for 8—10 minutes in an oven preheated to 180°C (350°F).

Allow the bread to cool for 1 minute before turning it out and slicing in half horizontally.

You can serve the bread just as it is, or toast on a sandwich press or under the grill (broiler).

Apple pie mug cake

A quick treat to satisfy a little craving is not as guilt laden as you think, if you are making my 5-minute apple pie mug cake. This cake is gluten and sugar free, and all you need to make it is a microwave!

½ green apple, peeled and grated

pinch ground cinnamon

pinch mixed spice

pinch ground ginger

3 tablespoons almond flour or almond meal

1 tablespoon inulin powder

1 egg

½ teaspoon baking powder

½ teaspoon pure vanilla extract

unsweetened coconut yoghurt to serve (optional)

pan-fried apples to serve (optional)

Place the grated apple, cinnamon, mixed spice and ground ginger into a large mug or ramekin, then microwave on high for 1 minute. Stir in the remaining ingredients, return the mug to the microwave and cook on high for a further 2 minutes.

Allow the cake to sit for 1 minute before turning out onto a little plate. Top with a spoon of coconut yoghurt and a few pan-fried apples (if using).

TIP I top my apple cake with unsweetened coconut yoghurt and some pan-fried apples. While both optional, they are wonderful!

TIP To make pan-fried apples: Slice a green apple half into pieces and place in a pan with a teaspoon of mixed spice and 1 teaspoon inulin powder. Cook for 4–5 minutes, stirring regularly until soft and golden.

Hot love

The original Hot Love was the invention of one my favourite bosses and business owners. In the late 1990s, I was the head chef of Merlot wine café in Auckland, New Zealand. Merlot was the brainchild of Martina Lutz, an impressive businesswoman whom I still consider as one of my friends, even though it's been 20 years since I last worked behind the stoves in her restaurants. Hot love was a simple dessert, mixing boutique ice cream and hot mixed sweetened berries. It has been crying out to be made into a healthy (though still boutique) recipe.

150 g (5¼ oz) frozen mixed berries

3 teaspoons inulin powder, plus extra for dusting

120 g (4¼ oz) unsweetened coconut yoghurt

Place the berries and 1½ teaspoons of inulin into a small saucepan on the stove. Heat gently until the berries have defrosted and warmed through. Don't allow the berries to come to the boil, because they will break up and become mushy.

Stir the remaining 1½ teaspoons of inulin through the yoghurt and, while the berries are still hot, spoon the yoghurt and berries into a bowl or glass, finishing with a light dusting on inulin on top.

Serve immediately.

Quick muffin bread

Sometimes a piece of bread is called for - this little treat is not only gluten free, it takes mere minutes to make! Use this as a healthy base for your poached eggs, toast until golden, smear avocado or my sugar-free berry jam over it, or layer with juicy tomatoes and a sprinkle of Himalayan salt.

½ tablespoon coconut flour

1 heaped tablespoon almond flour

½ teaspoon baking powder

1 egg

1 tablespoon water

½ teaspoon nutritional yeast (optional)

pinch Himalayan salt

Using a small microwaveable container or mug, whisk together the coconut flour, almond flour, baking powder, egg, water and nutritional yeast with a fork until free from lumps. Season with a pinch of salt.

Microwave on high for 90 seconds until the bread appears cooked and no longer looks doughy.

Allow the bread to sit for a minute then turn it out from the mug.

Serve whole or sliced in half. This bread also comes up really nicely when toasted.

TIP To make this recipe quickly, you will need a microwave. Alternatively, bake in a muffin tray lined with paper cases for 10–12 minutes in an oven preheated to 180°C (350°F).

Coconut chocolate mousse

A smooth silky mousse that hits all the spots, this creamy concoction is a dream come true. It uses no dairy or sugar, yet is sweet enough to serve to unsuspecting guests at your next dinner party. Yes, it's that good!

400 ml (14 fl oz) can coconut cream

2–3 tablespoons tablespoon inulin powder

2 tablespoons raw cacao powder, sifted

2 tablespoons grated vegan chocolate (page 215) (optional)

Leave the can of coconut cream undisturbed in the fridge overnight.

The next day, without shaking the can, carefully open it. Using a tablespoon, extract the solid cream at the top of the can without disturbing the watery liquid at the bottom. Remove as much as you can, putting the collected cream into a mixing bowl.

Sprinkle over the inulin powder and, using an electric whisk, whisk for 2 minutes or until thick and creamy.

Sprinkle over half the cacao powder and whisk into the mixture. Taste for flavour, adding more cacao or a bit more inulin powder if you desire a richer more chocolatey taste.

To serve, spoon into glasses and sprinkle with sugar-free grated chocolate (if using). You can also cover with cling film and store in the refrigerator for up to 1 day before serving.

TIP Start this recipe the day before you wish to serve it, because the can of coconut cream/milk needs to sit in the fridge overnight.

TIP Any left over coconut liquid can be saved and used in curries or sauces.

Homemade nori chips

The crunch and flavour make these snack treats irresistible! So easy to make, so healthy to chomp, so good for you nutritionally. These treats are a win-win in every situation!

4 sheets nori

Option 1

1 tablespoon water

4 pinches salt

Option 2

½ tablespoon tamari

4 pinches pure garlic powder

Option 3

½ tablespoon tamari

½ tablespoon sesame oil

1 teaspon white sesame seeds

Cut each sheet of nori into 6 even-sized rectangles.

Heat a pan on medium temperature and, depending on what flavour option you choose, brush the sheets with a tiny amount of the liquid.

Place 3–4 nori rectangles into the pan at once and sprinkle with your chosen toppings. Quickly cook the chips for 10–15 seconds on one side before flipping to cook on the other side. The chips are done when the colour of the nori darkens.

Remove from the pan and repeat the process until all the chips are cooked.

Enjoy immediately, because these snacks do not stay crisp for long. Moisture is their enemy so, if you plan to store them, do so in an airtight container with the bag of absorbent crystals from the original nori packet.

Dandy chai

I have long suffered with water and fluid retention. All the women on my mother's side of the family have suffered with this terribly - my childhood memories are filled with aunties and grandmas sitting with uncomfortable swollen legs, ankles and feet. Dandelion tea, I am delighted to say, has helped me immensely because it's a natural gentle diuretic. I especially enjoy drinking it after a plane trip to ease the swelling from long-haul flights. Now, I give you my recipe to create your own dandy chai, which is an even MORE delightful way to consume dandelion tea! Who doesn't love chai?

3 heaped tablespoons roasted dandelion tea blend
or
4 teabags dandelion tea

1 cinnamon quill

3 star anise

4 cloves

½ tablespoon finely grated fresh ginger

4 whole black peppercorns

2 cardamom pods, smashed with the flat side of a large knife

2 tablespoons inulin powder (optional)

lemon slices and mint leaves to serve (optional)

Into a pot add 1.1 litres (37 fl oz) of cold water, along with all ingredients except the inulin powder.

Stir the mixture a few times then bring the pot to a gentle simmer. Continue to simmer gently for 10 minutes then turn off the heat. Stir through the inulin powder (if using).

For hot tea: Strain the liquid to remove all the spices and serve hot with a slice of lemon.

For iced tea: Allow the liquid to cool. When cold, strain the liquid to remove all the spices. Serve over ice with a slice of lemon, a handful of mint leaves and a straw for sipping.

WORTH PRESERVING.

The secret of these tasty preserves is that they add flavour quickly and easily to every dish.

I make sure that I have several jars of pickles, cucumbers and onions in the cupboard or fridge, and they inspire me to create a healthy meal when I am tempted to try something less healthy.

You can use any jar with a screw top but always make sure you wash your jars in hot soapy water, or run them through a dishwasher, without any dishwasher detergent first. You can place them in a warm oven for about 10 minutes to dry off and to make sure that they are absolutely clean and dry before using.

Preserves

Pickled cucumbers

I have an unexplained desire to put food in jars! I adore the idea of pickling and preserving and giving food a different flavour and texture, plus it's the best way to make sure you don't let an abundance of cheap produce go to waste.

1 kg (2 lb 4 oz) Lebanese (short) cucumbers, cut into even rounds or large sticks

240 ml (8 fl oz) apple cider vinegar

240 ml (8 fl oz) white vinegar

480 ml (16½ fl oz) water

2 tablespoons Himalayan salt

2 teaspoons coriander seeds

2 teaspoons mustard seeds

2 teaspoons fennel seeds

2 large garlic cloves, peeled and thinly sliced

4 small thyme sprigs

Make the brine by gently heating the apple cider vinegar, white vinegar, water and salt in a pot until the salt is fully dissolved.

Place the coriander, mustard and fennel seeds in a small frying pan and dry-fry over medium heat for a couple of minutes, or until they are fragrant and lightly coloured.

Into 2–4 clean jars (depending on size) pack the sliced cucumbers and evenly distribute the toasted seeds, sliced garlic and thyme sprigs. Pour over the warm brine and place the lids on the jars.

Ideally, leave the pickles for 48 hours for the flavour to develop, but I am more than happy to eat them after only a few minutes!

These pickles will keep in your fridge for up to 3 months.

Quick zucchini pickles

The first time I encountered zucchini (courgette) pickles was in a cookbook written by the effervescent Alice Waters of Chez Panisse in California. Having spent the better part of my life thinking zucchinis had to be cooked, she opened my eyes to the quick preserving possibilities of many vegetables. I love the simplicity of these pickles and the punchy flavour, thanks to the fabulous spices.

3 tablespoons Himalayan salt

180 ml (6 fl oz) apple cider vinegar

180 ml (6 fl oz) water

1 teaspoon turmeric powder

1 teaspoon yellow mustard seeds

1 teaspoon fennel seeds

1 teaspoon cumin seeds

500 g (1 lb 2 oz) zucchini (courgette)

1 red onion

Place a pot over medium heat and add the salt, apple cider vinegar, water and turmeric. Bring to a gentle simmer, dissolving the salt.

Heat a small frying pan over medium–high heat and dry-fry the mustard, fennel and cumin seeds for 1 minute, or until the mustard seeds pop. Remove from the heat.

Using a mandolin slicer set on thin slice, slice the zucchini lengthways to get long, thin strips.

Peel and cut the red onion in half and slice the onion on the mandolin using the same thin slice setting.

Mix the two vegetables together, then pack them into 1–2 clean jars (depending on size) and evenly distribute the toasted seeds. Pour over the warm brine and place the lids on the jars.

Ideally, leave the pickles for 48 hours for the flavour to develop, although you can begin to consume them 30 minutes after pickling.

These pickles will last in your fridge for up to 1 month.

TIP I used a mandolin slicer (page 19) to get thin, even slices which is much easier, quicker and more effective than using a knife.

Delish pickled onions

I deliberated over what to name this recipe because I wanted to give it the kudos it so rightly deserves. I grew up fearing pickled onions - they were large complicated things, requiring you to pucker up before consuming. These pickled onions contain none of my unfortunate childhood memories. They are, in fact, so wonderfully balanced that they work just as well through a salad or served with a platter of cold sliced meats.

200 ml (7 fl oz) apple cider vinegar

125 g (4½ fl oz) inulin powder

1 teaspoon Himalayan salt

300 g (10½ oz) red or white onions, peeled and sliced into thick rounds

1 dried red chilli

Place the apple cider vinegar, inulin powder and salt in a saucepan and bring to the boil. Remove the liquid from the heat and allow it to cool.

Place the onions into a clean medium-sized jar then add the red chilli. Pour over the cooled pickling liquid and make sure the onions are fully submerged in the liquid.

Cover the jar with a tight-fitting lid and store in the refrigerator. Leave the onions to cure for 1 day before consuming. They can be stored for up to 3 months in the fridge.

TIP Don't throw away the liquid when you've eaten all the onions. Provided you use clean utensils every time you dip into the jar, you can make another round of onions using the same liquid! I make new onions almost every week because I absolutely adore them!

Preserved lemons

The flavour of these preserved lemons is incredibly good. So unlike raw lemons, the preserved version is exotic and packed full of flavour – a little goes a long way. And when I mean little, all you need to use to flavour your stew and tagines is a very small piece of the lemon skin, finely chopped.

6–8 lemons, well washed to remove any wax on the skin

2 lemons, juiced (optional)

150 g (5½ oz) Himalayan salt

Cut the tips off either ends of the lemons. Then using a sharp knife, cut the lemons lengthways through the middle starting at one end but DO NOT cut right through. The lemon should stay intact at one end.

Repeat this cut so that the lemon is cut into quarters but still intact at one end.

Carefully pull the lemon segments apart without breaking them from the base and fill the lemon cavity with salt.

Pack the filled lemons into the jar, squeezing as you go to extract the lemon juice. There should be enough lemon juice to cover the lemons. If not, add enough juice to completely cover the lemons.

Add any salt that may be leftover and top the jar with a clean lid. Place the jar at the back of the fridge and allow the lemons to preserve for a minimum of 3 weeks before using.

TIP I used a 1 litre (35 fl oz/4 cup) preserving jar to store my lemons. You can use one large sterilised jar or a couple of small ones with well-fitting lids.

TIP Preserved lemons can be used to help flavour stews, curries and tagines. You can sterilise the jar by boiling the jar for 5 minutes in a large pot of water. Carefully remove the jar from the hot water and allow it to drain on a clean tea towel before filling with the salted lemons.

VEGETABLE BASES.

These simple recipes will allow you to add the benefits of fresh vegetables to any meal.

Broccoli mash (which is a great source of vitamins K and C, folic acid, potassium and fibre) air-fried cauliflower and crunchy zucchini can be served with any meal, replacing far less healthy choices.

Veg

Cauliflower rice

A low-carb alternative to rice! I've given cooking methods for both oven and microwave below.

300–400 g (10½–14 oz) raw cauliflower florets

½ teaspoon nutmeg

½ teaspoon cumin

1 tablespoon finely chopped flat-leaf (Italian) parsley

1 tablespoon finely chopped mint

Cut the cauliflower florets into small pieces and add them to a food processor. Depending on the size of your food processor, you may have to work in batches as you don't want to overcrowd the bowl. Blend the cauliflower for 20–30 seconds, or until it resembles rice.

At this stage you can store the cauliflower rice in the fridge for up to 3 days, or you can freeze it in zip lock bags in the freezer for up to 2 months.

If using a microwave, combine the cauliflower rice with the nutmeg and cumin and cover in plastic wrap. Heat on high for 3 minutes, then season well with salt and pepper. Stir through the chopped parsley and mint.

If using an oven, preheat the oven to 200°C (400°F) and line a baking tray with baking paper. Mix the nutmeg and cumin through the cauliflower and lay the cauliflower out in a thin layer. Roast for 10–12 minutes, stirring halfway through the cooking time.

Season well with salt and pepper and mix through the chopped parsley and mint before serving.

Air fryer cauliflower

Crisp with a little crunch, these flavoursome cauliflower chips are cooked using an air fryer. They are easy and quick to make, plus they are big on taste.

1 teaspoon ground nutmeg

1 teaspoon paprika

1 teaspoon cumin powder

1 teaspoon pure garlic powder

½ teaspoon Himalayan salt

½ teaspoon freshly ground black pepper

4 tablespoons water

300–400 g (10½–14 oz) raw cauliflower florets, evenly cut

Mix together the nutmeg, paprika, cumin, garlic, salt and pepper. Drizzle the water over the cauliflower and ensure all the florets are a little damp. Sprinkle the cauliflower with the spices.

Preheat the air fryer to 200°C (400°F) for 2 minutes and lay the cauliflower in a single layer in the basket. You may need to work in batches depending on the size of your air fryer. Cook for 5–7 minutes until tender.

Cauliflower mash

This mash is wonderful! Use it as a base for a stew, with roasted meats or on top of a glorious cottage pie.

300–400 g (10½–14 oz) raw cauliflower florets

Himalayan salt and freshly ground black pepper

2 teaspoons finely chopped rosemary leaves

4 roasted garlic cloves, mashed (page 46)

½ teaspoon nutmeg

½ teaspoon cumin

Place the cauliflower florets in a pot with just enough water to cover the cauliflower, then season with a pinch of salt. Bring the water to the boil, then reduce the heat until the water is rapidly simmering. Cook the cauliflower for 12–15 minutes, or until very tender.

Drain the cooked water from the cauliflower very well. This step is important to make sure you get a smooth cauliflower mash or purée rather than a watery one. Shake the cauliflower well to ensure all the water is drained.

Blend the cauliflower until very smooth using a small food processor together with the rosemary leaves, roasted garlic, nutmeg and cumin. Season to taste with a little salt and pepper.

Zucchini noodles

Easy to make, if you have a spiraliser or mandolin slicer (page 19), and so incredibly versatile to use. Use 'zoodles' to replace spaghetti and noodles. Add to soups, quickly stir-fry or toss through a salad.

zucchini (courgette), peeled into noodles

Give the zucchini a light scrub under cold water.

Using your spiraliser or mandolin, peel the zucchini into noodles. You can also use a wide peeler and create ribbons, then thinly slice the ribbons into noodles with a sharp knife.

Use immediately or store, covered, in the fridge for up to 2 days.

TIP Perhaps my favourite way to have zucchini. Ribbons are a great way to avoid soggy zucchini noodles in a stir-fry.

Zucchini chips

We all like a bit of crunch in our life, especially if that crunch is 100% healthy with no added oils, sugar or fat. Made with nature's own thinly sliced zucchini, they are given the golden touch in a slow, cool oven before they are ready to be munched on and savoured. Could these be the ultimate healthy couch snack?

600 g (1 lb 5 oz) zucchini (courgette), thinly cut into 2–3 mm (⅛ in) slices using a mandolin or vegetable slicer

½ tablespoon Himalayan salt

1 tablespoon ground wakame (page 40)

1 tablespoon powdered garlic

Lay the zucchini slices in a single layer onto a couple of clean tea towels. Sprinkle the zucchini with the Himalayan salt and place another couple of clean towels on top of the zucchini. Leave to sit on the bench for 2 hours.

Press the top tea towel onto the zucchini for 1 minute to extract more moisture and leave the zucchini to sit for a further 1 hour. By the end of the 3 hours the bottom towels should be saturated with liquid, which is exactly what you want!

Preheat the oven to 90°C (195°F) with the shelves positioned as low to the bottom of the oven as possible.

Line 2 large wire racks with baking paper and lay the zucchini slices on them in a single layer. Sprinkle one rack of zucchini with the wakame and the other rack with the powdered garlic.

Bake the zucchini for 1 hour 20 minutes–1 hour 30 minutes, rotating the trays halfway through the cooking period so that they cook evenly. Your chips are done when they are crisp and golden and very crunchy. Serve immediately or cool briefly on the tray before storing in a small airtight container.

TIP Be prepared, this recipe does take a bit of time to sit and soak (3 hours) and the cook time is 1 hour and 20 minutes but the crunchy results are worth it.

TIP One of the main methods to getting a consistent crunchy chip is cutting the zucchini into even slices using a mandolin.

TIP Go easy with the seasoning. The zucchini shrinks and shrivels as it cooks and the flavour concentrates.

TIP The crunch in these chips does not last long. They need to be eaten straight away or as soon as they have cooled.

Broccoli rice

Broccoli rice is our mean, lean green friend! With so much flavour and vibrant colour, it's a great way to get more broccoli into your diet. I've given you cooking methods for both the oven and microwave below.

300–400 g (10½–14 oz) raw broccoli florets

Himalayan salt and freshly ground black pepper

Cut the broccoli florets into small pieces and add them to a food processor. Depending on the size of your food processor, you may have to work in batches as you don't want to overcrowd the bowl. Blend the broccoli for 20–30 seconds, or until it resembles rice.

At this stage you can store your broccoli rice in the fridge for up to 3 days, or you can freeze it in zip lock bags in the freezer for up to 2 months.

If you are using a microwave, cook the broccoli rice on high, covered in plastic wrap, for 3–4 minutes, then season well with salt and pepper.

If you are using the oven, preheat the oven to 200°C (400°F) and line a baking tray with baking paper. Lay the broccoli out in a thin layer and roast for 10–12 minutes, stirring halfway through the cooking time. Season well with salt and pepper before serving.

Index

Published in 2020 by Murdoch Books, an imprint of Allen & Unwin

Murdoch Books Australia
83 Alexander Street
Crows Nest NSW 2065
Phone: +61 (0)2 8425 0100
murdochbooks.com.au
info@murdochbooks.com.au

Murdoch Books UK
Ormond House
26–27 Boswell Street
London WC1N 3JZ
Phone: +44 (0) 20 8785 5995
murdochbooks.co.uk
info@murdochbooks.co.uk

For corporate orders and custom publishing, contact our business development team at
salesenquiries@murdochbooks.com.au

Publisher: Corinne Roberts
Editorial Manager: James Mills-Hicks
Design Manager: Kristy Allen
Designer: Trisha Garner
Editors: Gordana Trifunovic, Audra Barclay, Jess Cox
Photographer: Rebecca Elliott
Illustrator: Trisha Garner
Production Director: Lou Playfair

ISBN 978 1 922351272 Australia
ISBN 978 1 91166 813 8 UK

 A catalogue record for this
book is available from the
National Library of Australia

Printed by C & C Offset Printing Co. Ltd., China

IMPORTANT: Those who might be at risk from the effects of salmonella poisoning (the elderly, pregnant women, young children
and those suffering from immune deficiency diseases) should consult their doctor with any concerns about eating raw eggs.

OVEN GUIDE: You may find cooking times vary depending on the oven you are using. For fan-forced ovens, as a general rule,
set the oven temperature to 20°C (70°F) lower than indicated in the recipe.

10 9 8 7 6 5 4 3 2 1

 The paper in this book is FSC® certified.
FSC® promotes environmentally responsible,
socially beneficial and economically viable
management of the world's forests.